Beyond Universities:
A New Republic of
the Intellect

SIR DOUGLAS HAGUE, CBE

IEA

Published by
INSTITUTE OF ECONOMIC AFFAIRS
1991

First published in April 1991

by

THE INSTITUTE OF ECONOMIC AFFAIRS
2 Lord North Street, Westminster,
London SW1P 3LB

© THE INSTITUTE OF ECONOMIC AFFAIRS 1991

Hobart Paper 115

ISSN 0073-2818
ISBN 0-255 36244-7

The Institute gratefully acknowledges financial support for its publications programme and other work from a generous benefaction by the late Alec and Beryl Warren.

Printed in Great Britain by
GORON PRO-PRINT CO LTD
6 Marlborough Road, Churchill Industrial Estate, Lancing, W. Sussex
Text set in Berthold Baskerville

CONTENTS

[3]

FOREWORD

The *Hobart Papers* are intended to provide a stream of independent, authoritative and lucid analyses to the understanding and application of micro-economics to private and government activity. The central theme has been the optimum use of scarce resources in a market economy, within an appropriate legal framework. Although higher education is viewed as a merit good, the same basic economic principles should apply to the provision of this service.

The major period of growth of the 'Red Brick' universities occurred during the early 1960s when economic wisdom consisted of interventionism, paternalism, corporatism and Keynesianism. It was against this background that the Robbins Report in 1963 advocated the expansion of higher education in Britain.

In a previous Hobart Paper (No. 102), *Whose Business?*, by Brian Griffiths and Hugh Murray, the authors argued that universities operated under a common system which institutionalised important restrictive practices. The universities have traditionally operated in a cartel whose output has been regulated by government. The individual firms (i.e. universities) are allocated quotas of students by government, with fees and salaries set in ways that are typical of a classic cartel. The university cartel is underpinned by a further monopoly, granted as of right to each university. In the UK, nobody can award degrees unless empowered to do so by royal charter or by the Secretary of State for Education and Science.

Professor Sir Douglas Hague takes this analysis a stage further by stating that the current stage of economic development is strongly based on the acquisition, analysis and transmission of information and on its application. Universities will therefore be forced to share, or even give up, part of their rôle as repositories of information and as power-houses for ideas, transmitted through teaching and writing.

The technological revolution that has taken place in the information and communications industries is bound to transform the way in which universities carry out traditional

[5]

functions, such as teaching. Further, these technologies, new ways of thinking and the consequent development of knowledge businesses engaged in activities like research, consultancy and training, will lead to increasing competition for the universities from competitors in such organisations. It will come both from the services they offer and from the salaries they pay. To compete, universities will have to organise and operate themselves in ways that are more like those of the knowledge-related industries. Indeed, they may be forced to form alliances with these newcomers if they are to continue with activities which previously they had assumed were theirs by right.

The process of economic development in the UK reached a paradoxical position in the 1980s. We had reached a record level of post-war unemployment at a time when the economy was also suffering from chronic skills shortages in certain sectors of industry. In this richly original and forward looking *Hobart Paper*, Professor Sir Douglas Hague identifies the challenges which universities will have to meet; if these can be overcome, universities should be able to survive both as competitors and complements of the knowledge industries over the coming decades.

The constitution of the Institute of Economic Affairs requires that all Trustees, Directors and Advisory Council members dissociate themselves from the analysis and conclusions of its authors but they commend this thought-provoking *Hobart Paper* by Professor Sir Douglas Hague. The Institute has, for the past three decades, pioneered research and publications in the political economy of education and will continue to do so since it is so fundamental to the prosperity of current and future generations.

April 1991   WALTER ALLAN

AUTHOR'S PREFACE AND ACKNOWLEDGEMENTS

In his review of Peter Hennessy's book on *Whitehall*, Professor George Jones of the London School of Economics makes a surprising statement.[1] Having called the work 'a remarkable achievement, a tribute to Hennessy's assiduity and enthusiasm', he goes on: 'No full-time academic, distracted from research by administrative chores, teaching and supervision, could have written this book.' He attributes Peter Hennessy's ability to do so to 'years of reporting on the Civil Service with privileged access to the denizens of Whitehall', to use of his own articles and broadcasts, and to the fact that 'he has burrowed deeply into the Public Record Office'.

Professor Jones implies that the best preparation for becoming a successful scholar is now not necessarily a post in a university. In Peter Hennessy's case, a period in journalism followed by the decision to become a freelance writer and broadcaster has left Peter poised between the media, the universities and the knowledge industries.

I did not see Professor Jones's review until I had almost finished this paper, but it highlights the type of change I discuss.

There are more clever, well-educated people outside the universities than there ever have been. Many work outside the educational field, in organisations large or small. Others, like Peter Hennessy, are freelances. All are potential allies and potential competitors of universities.

Professor Jones's comments personalise and therefore dramatise the change which is taking place in the relative position of the universities. The growing reservoir of talent outside them, together with the growing power of information and communications technology, face universities throughout the world with the most far-reaching change in their prospects that they have ever experienced. This *Hobart Paper* considers the implications of that change for universities.

I am grateful to Dr Hennessy and to Mr Norman Strauss for reading my manuscript and for making helpful suggestions and

[1] Peter Hennessy, *Whitehall*, London: Secker & Warburg, 1989. Review by George Jones is in *Government and Opposition*, Summer 1990.

comments. I add the usual disclaimer, absolving them from any responsibility for the views I have expressed. They are mine alone.

I also thank Mrs Denise Edwards for turning a messy manuscript into a first-rate typescript with her customary speed and skill. Not least, I thank her for doing most of the work at a time of year better devoted to sport or holidays.

March 1991   D.H.

THE AUTHOR

SIR DOUGLAS HAGUE, CBE, is an Associate Fellow of Templeton College, Oxford, and Honorary Visiting Professor at Imperial College, London, and at Manchester Business School, where he was previously Professor of Managerial Economics (1965-81) and Deputy Director (1978-81). His previous academic appointments included: Professor of Economics, University of Sheffield (1957-63); Professor of Applied Economics, University of Manchester (1963-65). After Manchester Business School he was Professorial Fellow at the Oxford Centre for Management Studies (1981-83), before his appointment as Chairman of the Economic and Social Research Council (1983-87).

Professor Hague has been a Director of the Laird Group (1972-75), a Member of the Price Commission (1973-78, Deputy Chairman, 1977-78), and Adviser to the Prime Minister's Policy Unit (1979-83). He is a director of CRT Group plc, and Chairman of Corporate Positioning Services. He was appointed CBE in 1978 and knighted in 1982.

His publications include: two textbooks written with A. W. Stonier: *A Textbook of Economic Theory* (1953), and *The Essentials of Economics* (1955); *Managerial Economics* (1969); (with Bruce L. R. Smith) *The Dilemma of Accountability in Modern Government* (1971); (with W. J. M. Mackenzie and A. Barker) *Public Policy and Private Interests: The Institutions of Compromise* (1975); (with Geoffrey Wilkinson) *The IRC—An Experiment in Industrial Intervention* (1982); (with Peter Hennessy) *How Adolf Hitler Reformed Whitehall* (1985).

[8]

I. INTRODUCTION

In a nutshell, the thesis of my *Hobart Paper* is that the current stage of economic development is strongly based on the acquisition, analysis and transmission of information and on its application. Universities will therefore be forced to share, or even to give up part of their rôle as repositories of information and as power-houses for ideas, transmitted through teaching and writing.

First, the technological innovations of the information and communications revolution are bound to transform the way universities carry out traditional functions, especially teaching. Second, these technologies, new ways of thinking and the consequent development of knowledge businesses engaged in activities like research, consultancy and training, will lead to increasing competition for the universities from competitors in such organisations. It will come both from the services they offer and from the salaries they pay. To compete, universities will have to organise and operate in ways more like those of knowledge businesses themselves. Indeed, they will often have to form alliances with these newcomers if they are to go on engaging in activities which they have supposed were their own, as if by right.

This *Paper* may therefore be seen as a frontal attack on the contemporary university. If it is, that will miss its point. I do have reservations about the way in which British universities sought to adapt structures which may have been appropriate in the 1960s so that they would fit the 1980s, but the adaptation then required was not great. The world of the 1990s and 2000s will be radically different from that of the 1980s in precisely the field which universities have traditionally seen as central to what they do: the generation, storage and dissemination of knowledge. It is because I *am* keen that the universities should survive both as competitors and complements of the knowledge industries that in this *Paper* I try to identify for universities the challenges which they will meet in the coming decades. I do so not in the hope that the universities may fail in meeting them, but that they may succeed.

II. BACKGROUND: THE DEVELOPMENT OF THE KNOWLEDGE INDUSTRIES

The process of economic development in all advanced countries follows a similar path and the UK is no exception. In Britain, a period when agriculture predominated gave way in the late 18th and 19th centuries to the Industrial Revolution. Manufacturing then dominated the economy for over 100 years. Employment in manufacturing reached its peak around 1970 when it accounted for some eight million people. The figure is now about five million. During the 1970s, British economic policy sought to cushion manufacturing against competitive pressures—not least to prevent rising unemployment. Partly because Britain's adjustment to changing markets and technology was thereby delayed, there was a rapid fall in manufacturing output and employment in the early 1980s. It was followed by a recovery in output, but not employment.

In 1974, 7·9 million people were employed in manufacturing and represented 32 per cent of the UK labour force. In 1979 the figure was still 31 per cent, but the more bracing economic climate of the 1980s has meant that only 20 per cent of the workforce is now in manufacturing.

It is important to recognise that this is not exceptional. Similar proportions of the labour force are employed in manufacturing in major Western European economies like France, Italy, Belgium, Switzerland, Sweden—and fewer (17 per cent) in the Netherlands. The USA and Canada have less than 20 per cent, and even Japan, whose economic performance is viewed with awe by most Western Europeans, has only some 24 per cent of its workers in manufacturing.

We can now expect manufacturing *output* to stabilise at its present proportion—roughly one-quarter—of GDP: the UK's position is typical of that in our kind of economy. Over time, however, the proportion of *employed people* working in manufacturing will continue to fall, not least because computerised manufacturing systems will take over from people engaged in shopfloor production.

This summary must be qualified in an important respect.

Many manufacturing—and indeed non-manufacturing—companies are now putting out increasing proportions of their activities to a 'contractual fringe' of individuals and small businesses who provide them with a range of services from cleaning and transport to consultancy, training and financial services, such as the management of pension funds. The number of people working *for* manufacturing businesses, as distinct from those working *in* them, has fallen by less than the figures quoted above suggest, though the importance of this should not be exaggerated. A study of this phenomenon by G. F. Ray of the National Institute of Economic and Social Research, in 1986, found it impossible to quantify what had happened over the decade 1973-83.[1] He did, however, point to a rise in expenditure by manufacturing businesses on business and professional services from 3 per cent to nearly 6 per cent of gross manufacturing output between 1973 and 1983, and the 'fringe' has certainly grown substantially since then.

I emphasise the position in manufacturing because it has become a British obsession to see the decline in manufacturing employment as a pathological phenomenon. The *speed* of the decline in the 1980s was dramatic but resulted, in part at least, from the determination to prevent any fall in the 1970s. At the time, it was thought that this would then have to be reversed and so was unnecessary. Yet there clearly *was* something pathological about the situation in 1974 when 32 per cent of the labour force was engaged in manufacturing but produced only 27 per cent of British output—a situation which was unsustainable if the UK wanted to achieve levels of productivity and therefore standards of living like those of our major competitors.

The Information Revolution

We are now moving into a new phase. With less than a quarter of Britons working in agriculture and manufacturing together, a major source of both employment and economic development will in future be the information revolution. This concept is now being extended to cover related developments in telecommunications under the heading 'the information and communications revolution'. In this *Paper*, we examine the knowledge industries, which are broader still.

The problem with the notion of the Information Revolution

[1] George F. Ray, 'Services for Manufacturing', *National Institute Economic Review*, August 1986, p. 30.

(or even the information and communications revolution) was that it over-emphasised the importance of technology. Developments in computers have, of course, been staggering. They have transformed our ability to manipulate large amounts of data and to present it to individuals and to small and large groups. Computer manufacturers insist that although computers are already cheap by earlier standards, there will *each year* be a 30-40 per cent reduction in *real* terms in the cost of computers during the 1990s, while what computers can do will develop dramatically over the decade. That decade will also see new fruits of the communications revolution in an increasing ability to transmit messages, data and pictures to the farthest parts of the world at steadily decreasing cost. Video conferencing, where individuals and small groups will be able not merely to speak to each other but to watch each other on television monitors transmitting high-quality pictures via satellites or along optical fibres, will also become steadily cheaper as the decade progresses. Yet, dramatic as they are, even these developments will represent no more than the *production* end of the knowledge society.

This new phase of economic development, during which we are creating the knowledge society, is one where a growing percentage of the population will be handling information or, more broadly, knowledge. Where this is done with computers, much of the work will become relatively routine—though achieving computing miracles by the standards even of the 1960s. The most exciting developments will be where human brains—often, it is true, supported by computers or other new technologies—work out radically new ways of understanding situations and events, solving problems, running organisations and transmitting knowledge. The knowledge society will have a huge impact on life and work and much of that impact will fall on the universities.

Private Knowledge Business: The Competitive Threat

To restate the main arguments, the theme of my *Paper* is this: in the 1990s and 2000s, people *outside* the universities will increasingly be working in similar ways and with similar talents to those within; and they will often do so more innovatively and with greater vigour, because they will come to what they do untrammelled by academic traditions, preconceptions and institutions. The pioneers of the knowledge society will increasingly be able to compete with the universities and, increasingly, will

[12]

do so. Since most British universities are in the public sector and most knowledge businesses are in the private sector, this will be a battle in which the private sector will threaten some of the public sector's most entrenched monopolies.

To avoid being driven out of activities which they have imagined their own by right, the universities will have to make substantial changes in what they do and how they do it. Where they find that difficult, one solution will be to form alliances with the interlopers. Increasingly, the choice will be alliance or annihilation.

There is also an important subsidiary thesis. We cannot make sense of the unfolding story of economic development unless we bear continuously in mind how it proceeds. In any activity or organisation, the real incomes of those who work in it—their standards of living—rise over time. This is the normal outcome of economic development. But to be able to pay increasing real wages, organisations have to ensure that there is a corresponding increase in output per person employed. Some of that increased productivity comes from organising more effectively. The way that any organisation produces the goods or services it offers has to change; the ratio of highly-paid to less well-paid people may have to change; but the biggest source of extra output per person employed is often more capital equipment per person. This was true even in the 18th and 19th centuries and will be even more true in the highly technological world of the late 20th and early 21st centuries. As a senior businessman volunteered to me recently: universities will have to be like businesses and learn to pay twice as much to half as many people. Put so tersely, this is over-simplified, but it highlights a key issue.

As the knowledge society develops, those who work in universities cannot be immune from this kind of pressure—although, to listen to them, many believe that they are. When universities were relatively small and when real incomes over the whole economy were much lower than they are now, the government could finance the activities of the universities without much difficulty. With big universities, and with so many other calls on public money, higher pay for academics must mean what it does in the rest of the economy: fewer people on locally agreed pay scales, better organised and managed and backed up by more technology.

Virtually no academic will allow the argument in the previous paragraph to pass unchallenged. If change in universities could be achieved only by debate in which the opponents of my view had to be convinced—that view would have a lean time. That is, however, not the whole story. Two forces—at least—will work either to change the academics, or to outflank them.

First, as I have already indicated, there will be the innovators of the knowledge society—not simply in terms of what they do but in terms of what they *can* do, and what they are paid for doing it. To be rewarded similarly, academics will *have* to change. Secondly, pressures for change will receive increasing support from the fact that the knowledge society draws on information and *communications* technology. It will provide an expanding range of artefacts which will transform what can be done, especially in teaching.

A Republic of the Intellect

For universities, permeability is the key. The more the universities are permeable and the more the knowledge industries and all citizens who embrace intellectual pursuits and causes come within them, the more successful they will be. The best universities of the 21st century will bring together brain-power *where it is*, not where it can be institutionalised. The aim must be to create a republic of the intellect open to all, whose natural constituency will be those who keep themselves intellectually aware throughout their lives. That constituency must be heavily represented in the knowledge industries. The successful university of the 21st century *cannot* be an academic bunker; it will have to be permeable.

There is another influence on universities—the Universities Funding Council (UFC)—but as I shall explain, and as recent events show, such a bureaucracy is unlikely to stimulate effective innovation in a period of dramatic change.

Fortunately it is not *only* universities which can establish permeable organisations, though they are splendidly placed to do so. Businesses in the knowledge industries will be able—and should be encouraged—to establish their own 'universities', quite apart from forming alliances with existing ones. It is therefore important that academics should not write-off businessmen as 'thick' and unable to compete or collaborate intelligently.

One problem in the UK is that we often find it hard to get beyond Ealing Comedy caricatures. We are uniquely prone to this—a proclivity assisted by our unrivalled British ability to

[14]

partition society by education, profession, class and so on. Caricatures touch our imagination.

Hence, every academic is long-haired, gazing continually into an empty blue sky, and unable to run anything. By contrast, every businessman is living in Pinner; what little passion there is in him is reserved for the tennis court; and he brings to the conduct of his enterprise the fertile imagination of an actuary.

All academics are like characters from *Lucky Jim* or the *History Man*. All civil servants are from *Yes, Minister*; all scientists are Dr Strangeloves, planning to blow up the world. All businessmen, in turn, are dreamed up by John Braine. This would not matter if we simply laughed, but we—at least half of us—seem to believe it all. It is time for us to stop.

Put as tersely as possible, then, my argument will be this: Knowledge is permeable; technology is universal; universities are impermeable; the universities' regulator is set in concrete. Something's got to give.

III. THE UNIVERSITIES

(a) Some Basics

Universities have two main rôles—teaching and research—and a subsidiary but a growing one in consultancy. Many individual academics also engage in freelance writing, consultancy and so on.

In the UK, the teaching rôle of universities has traditionally required them to educate a relatively small proportion of the population, currently about 13 per cent of those leaving school. They prepare these students for first degrees which the universities themselves award. While many university degrees provide a broad and high-level education, especially in arts subjects, those in fields like medicine, technology, business and some branches of science and, perhaps, law are best seen as providing training rather than education. The social sciences—including economics—occupy an intermediate position in this spectrum.

Students for higher research degrees—master's or doctor's—are supervised by one or more academics. Especially in arts and social science subjects, many master's degrees and most doctorates are obtained by writing a thesis, with little or no formal training in research being given. True, many master's degrees are awarded for formal course work only but, while there is formal training for *some* master's degree students who write a thesis, this is still the exception rather than the rule with PhDs, especially in arts and social science.

Students working for degrees by writing theses receive variable treatment from their supervisors. Many supervisors take their rôle extremely seriously, although a minority rarely meet their students and appear largely unconcerned with their progress. There is a spectrum between these extremes. Not surprisingly, theses often take considerably longer to complete than the prescribed period, which is usually a year or two for a master's degree, but up to three or four for a doctorate. Many are not completed at all. In 1985, while I was its Chairman, the Economic and Social Research Council (ESRC) was at any one time funding some 1,200 students working towards PhDs, each for up to three years. The Council decided that it could not go on tolerating a situation where about half of these students *never* obtained a PhD, however much time they were allowed. The Council's convention had been that each student must submit a thesis for examination within four years. In 1984, as few as 25 per cent actually did.

Minimum Submission Rate for Theses

To force improvement, the Council set a minimum 'submission rate', namely a proportion of theses which had to be completed and handed in within four years. The cut-off percentage began at 10 per cent, has been steadily raised, and will be 50 per cent from 1991. Universities not achieving this rate are denied ESRC support for PhD students for three years. After that they have to show that they have made more satisfactory arrangements before their PhD students are supported again. Despite initial howls of protest and claims that improvement was impossible, there has been change in two ways.

First, the average 'submission rate' rose from 25 per cent in 1984 to 55 per cent in 1989, with a number of universities achieving rates around 100 per cent: and there has been a rise rather than a fall in quality. The biggest change seems to have been that the scope of theses has been reduced, which was the intention. Secondly, to achieve this, most universities have improved the arrangements they make for training and supervising doctoral students. In the best universities, they are now extremely good. The ESRC is also beginning to insist that universities must provide PhD students with adequate research training *before* allowing them to begin research for doctoral degrees.

Unfortunately, some large institutions continue merely to scrape past this cut-off rate, notably the London School of Economics and the Universities of Manchester and Oxford. (Cambridge University fell below that rate in 1989 and its students are therefore not being supported at present.) The 50 per cent cut-off rate will hit all three institutions unless they improve their performance.

In future, individual departments will be monitored and universities asked to specify those departments they no longer wish to see recognised by the ESRC for support. (I hope that one piece of research the ESRC will finance will then be into the implications of its sanctions for the numbers of PhD students and

[17]

for the scope and quality of their theses, not least in departments debarred from ESRC support by their own universities.) To obtain ESRC recognition the remaining departments will have to show the ESRC that the arrangements they make for PhD students are acceptable. After 1991, such a department will lose ESRC grants if its students fail to pass the 'cut-off' rate for submissions and not the whole social science faculty, as at present.

The conclusion from this episode is that while universities take seriously their rôle in training students for first degrees, and perhaps master's degrees, their treatment of doctoral students—especially in the arts and social sciences—has often been demonstrably unsatisfactory. Improvement has had to be forced on them and, as the evidence for the LSE, Manchester and Oxford cited above shows, it does not always happen even then.

The Best Way to Train Researchers?

This leaves to one side the question whether the best way to train men and women in their early 20's to become teachers, researchers, or anything else, is to require them to embark as PhD students on a major research work in a specialised field. Whatever academics say, only a small proportion of theses are read with significant benefit by other people and the small number which are could be published as books, if need be with Research Council support for the really able researcher. Instead of requiring a major piece of writing, a PhD in these fields should be much more like one in science.

Science, technology and medical students working for higher degrees appear to be much better treated. Even there, however, some universities were not achieving the relatively simple target of 50 per cent of government-funded students handing in their completed work within four years until the Science and Engineering Research Council took action in 1988 on similar lines to the ESRC. The reason for better performance seems to be partly that more of these PhDs share laboratories with other students, and indeed academic staff, avoiding the isolation in which too many arts and social science students work. Perhaps more important, the typical PhD in science tackles a relatively small and clearly defined topic. The typical social-science student—at least in my experience—begins a PhD convinced that he or she can in four years carry out a major and original research task on a scale which, if not representing a life's work, would keep a first-rate scholar occupied for several years. Unless assisted by a supervisor who is prepared to exert helpful discipline, not least in forcing the student to begin his writing *soon*, the average social science student is from the very beginning faced with an impossible task and, potentially, a demoralising one.

The other activities of academics which I intend to cover range over an enormous field: writing books and articles; broadcasting; consultancy (paid or unpaid) for governments, politicians, businesses, banks, etc. No-one knows, and probably no-one can accurately guess, how much time they take; but it is clearly substantial for a large minority of academics. Nor does anyone know how far 'consultancy on the side', and indeed research, detracts from the teaching of first-degree students and, more particularly, the supervision of those working for higher degrees.

In this *Paper* a major concern is with consultancy proper—with work carried out for payment, which provides analysis or advice to businesses or other organisations. Whether organised by the university itself—which then decides how to use the money earned—or by freelance individuals or groups from the universities, who keep the reward for themselves, consultancy is important to my argument. It is the field where there is at present most competition and/or collaboration between the universities and the knowledge industries.

As well as people—the students they teach and the academics and others who work in them—the universities have physical assets, buildings, teaching rooms, laboratories, workshops and, if they have medical faculties, hospitals, dental schools, and so on. Especially for the arts and social sciences, they provide libraries.

(b) Some Statistics

Individual British universities are, in principle, autonomous bodies with a good deal of freedom in the way they operate. In practice, that freedom is constrained in various ways. Before considering those constraints, we look briefly at the spread of activities in British universities and the ways they are financed. In 1987-88, the total recurrent income of British universities was just over £2,700 million. About 55 per cent of this (£1,482 million) came from central government via the University Grants Committee, replaced in 1989 by the Universities Funding Council (UFC). A further £346 million came from the tuition fees of students, a large proportion of it being paid for them by the local authorities in whose areas they lived.

The universities also received £530 million in research grants and contracts, about half of which (£277 million) came from central government, or from the five Government-financed Research Councils. About one-tenth (£78 million) was provided by industry. United Kingdom charities gave £109 million, a great deal of it for medical research.

The universities spent a little over £2,000 million on current account. Some 56 per cent (£1,118 million) went on supporting academic departments; £375 million on maintaining premises; £97 million on libraries; £87 million on other academic services; and £154 million on administrative and central services. Of the £1,118 million going on academic departments, a little over half (£670 million) was for science, £180 million for clinical work and £360 million for arts, including social science and law.

In 1987-88 there were 56,000 full-time academic and 'academic-related' staff, together with 258,000 undergraduates and 88,000 postgraduates—a total of 346,000 students.

There is more than one way of calculating the number of universities in the UK depending, for example, on whether one counts every individual college in Oxford, Cambridge and London separately. The official statistics distinguish 53 universities: 36 in England, seven in Wales, eight in Scotland, and two in Northern Ireland.

On average, they receive 55 per cent of their income from the Exchequer, but there is variation in this proportion. For example, the London Business School and Manchester Business School, which obtain large amounts of money from courses run for businessmen, obtained 49 per cent and 27 per cent respectively of their recurrent income from the Exchequer during 1987-88. Manchester Business School, in particular, has virtually become a private institution. At the other end of the scale, the University of Ulster relied on the Exchequer for nearly 76 per cent of total recurrent income, St David's College at Lampeter 69 per cent, Queens University, Belfast 67 per cent, East Anglia 66 per cent, Exeter 65 per cent, Hull 64 per cent and St Andrews 63 per cent.

The Distribution of Research Grants

One reason for this variation is that universities receive very different amounts from research grants and contracts. On average, the 53 obtain just over 19 per cent of their recurrent income in this way. Apart from the University of Wales College of Medicine, which is a special case, Oxford had the highest percentage, at nearly 29 per cent, followed by UMIST, London and Southampton (all somewhat over 25 per cent), Cambridge (24 per cent), Surrey (23 per cent), and Loughborough (22 per cent). At the bottom end were Lampeter and the University of Ulster with 6 per cent, Hull 8 per cent, City University 9 per cent and Salford 10 per cent. There is clearly some geographical pattern to this in the sense that, while research grants and contracts accounted for 20 per cent of recurrent income in England, they represented only 8½ per cent in Northern Ireland, 15 per cent in Wales and 18 per cent in Scotland. There does seem to be a North/South (and Welsh) divide.

There is less geographical difference for other forms of income, which cover receipts from running special and short courses together with those from training, consultancy and other related work for the National Health Service and central government. For the UK as a whole, this represented 6½ per cent of recurrent income: nearly 7 per cent for England and Wales, 6 per cent for Scotland and 5½ per cent for Northern Ireland.

Other Activities

Because ours is now a knowledge society and because knowledge depreciates steadily as time passes, continuing education is becoming increasingly important as the knowledge revolution proceeds. There is a dichotomy here. Some universities, for example Cambridge, concentrate such activity in extra-mural departments. Others (for example, Lancaster, UMIST, St David's, Lampeter and Heriot-Watt) have little or no extra-mural activity and organise such programmes through other university departments. This distinction is, of course, one of form rather than substance.

With work carried out for government departments, the universities which obtained most income from this source were: Salford (£2·8 million), which puts it well ahead of Queens University, Belfast (£1·7 million), itself well ahead of the best of the rest, namely London (£1·1 million), Manchester (£1·0 million), and the University of Wales College of Medicine (£0·4 million). Many universities earn a good deal of income from training programmes they run for the National Health Service, quite apart from its support of work in medical faculties.

Universities clearly specialise to some extent in what they do, but those with the broadest spread of activities are Birmingham, Bristol, Cambridge, City, London, Oxford, Salford, Sheffield, Southampton, Surrey, Warwick, University of Wales College of Medicine, Aberdeen, Edinburgh, Glasgow, Heriot-Watt and Queens University, Belfast. That is, 17 out of 53—about a third.

The other 36 universities concentrate on a narrower range of activities, especially undergraduate and postgraduate teaching. On average, about 81 per cent of their income takes the form of recurrent grants intended to cover such activities.

(c) Interlocking Monopolies

Central to my argument is the fact that the universities in the UK have built up an entrenched position, based on a number of monopolies, some natural and some artificial. Some of these are being eroded as the knowledge revolution proceeds; others remain. The biggest monopoly is of brain-power or, perhaps more accurately, brain-power specialising in academic activities. Most of these brains are used only in specialised academic ways—a self-imposed cultural limitation.

There have always been clever people—some of them much cleverer people—outside the universities, especially in the learned professions and in the civil service. But most have never devoted more than a fraction of their time to teaching or research—or indeed consultancy. When they have, they have often done so by giving or selling their time to universities. Examples are lawyers and accountants teaching professional subjects, industrialists speaking to business schools, and so on.

In research, too, the universities have been able very much—perhaps too much—to keep themselves to themselves. Universities account for much the greater proportion of *their* kind of research. People in the professions, the civil service, industry and commerce interested in similar topics, in most fields, account for only a small proportion of the papers written in the more academic journals. They also make little contribution to what the general public would see as the influential ideas in each field. Medicine is perhaps something of an exception, but the boundaries between what is inside and what outside the university's medical faculty have always been blurred.

Some recent developments enable us to glimpse the future. For example, law firms are now financing university chairs and seconding their partners to them in order to lecture. In effect, they are *buying* teaching posts. That must be something for universities, most of which are short of money, to ponder.

Similarly, some companies' research laboratories have established fruitful relationships with universities, including exchanges of staff.

In consultancy, only in very specialised fields have universities held even limited monopolies. The question, for this *Paper*, is what is happening to those limited monopolies as the knowledge revolution proceeds.

The second monopoly of the universities has been traditionally in certain kinds of facilities: in lecture and seminar rooms; in some kinds of equipment; and, above all, in libraries. Again, the monopoly has been stronger in some of the university's rôles than others. While their teaching facilities are no longer always as modern as they might wish, the universities are nevertheless strongly placed in being able to educate large numbers of students in reasonable comfort. That pre-eminence diminishes as one moves into research and, especially, into development work and consultancy. Nevertheless, in scientific research the position of the universities is strong; in the arts and the social sciences, the average research student would be hard put to work successfully without a university library as a base.

Natural and Institutionalised Monopolies

These monopoly elements may be described as giving *natural* monopolies in the sense that they are inherent in the realities of university education, though those realities are changing. They are, however, buttressed by man-made arrangements which derive from the way in which British governments support the universities.

Although there is clearly a considerable degree of diversity among universities, they operate under a common system which institutionalises important restrictive practices. As Brian Griffiths and Hugh Murray pointed out in 1985 in *Whose Business?*,[1] the universities have traditionally operated in a cartel whose output has been regulated by government. The individual 'firms' (i.e. universities) were allocated quotas of students by government, and fees and salaries were set in ways that were typical of a classic cartel. Some of the activities of the cartel are now less regulated though, as we shall see, attempts to move towards

[1] Brian Griffiths and Hugh Murray, *Whose Business?*, Hobart Paper 102, London: Institute of Economic Affairs, 1985.

competitive bidding for students have run into difficulty. But the rôle of the state remains essentially unchanged.

The university cartel is underpinned by a further man-made monopoly, granted as of right to each university. In the UK, nobody can award degrees unless empowered to do so by royal charter or by the Secretary of State for Education and Science. Unless eased, as it could be by wider exercise of his powers by the Secretary of State for Education and Science, this monopoly could over time inhibit the development of a fruitful competitive relationship between the universities and the knowledge industries, at least so far as teaching for degrees is concerned.

A significant easing of that monopoly took place when the Council for National Academic Awards (CNAA) was established in 1964 and given the power to approve the granting of CNAA degrees, by non-university organisations approved by the Council. Until recently, all of these organisations were public-sector colleges of various kinds, often polytechnics. As a result, the monopoly powers of universities are a little weaker than they were, though the monopoly over the award of degrees still remains largely confined to the public sector.

By late 1990, the CNAA had permitted the award of degrees to students on one or two degree programmes organised jointly by private businesses and polytechnics. This is an important move towards weakening their monopoly which has buttressed the position of the universities and polytechnics during the 20th century, and in time the rôle of business in higher education must grow. No service businesses are yet playing a part in these business/polytechnic partnerships but I look forward to the entry of more, smaller knowledge businesses over the next decade.

In October 1990, there was a small but perhaps significant development. British Telecom was given the right to train and assess its own employees who study for its equivalent to the Diploma in Management Studies. I hope that this is a significant omen in two senses. First, I hope it is a sign of the way the economy, and higher education, is developing that the firm concerned was British Telecom. Second, I hope that before long British Telecom, or a similar company, will be allowed to run degree as well as diploma programmes.

The ostensible reason for restricting the power to award degrees very largely to universities and polytechnics is that this maintains quality by guaranteeing that only institutions with 'acceptable' standards can do so. In reality, as we shall see, the system ensures rather that degrees awarded by the least-prestigious institutions are acceptable because they—indeed, *all* degrees—match the current views, on content and standards, of a sheltered academic profession.

The bureaucracy that supervises the universities can do little to ensure that *high* standards are reached, though that is not the real problem. The problem is that since most universities are singularly bad at innovation, the system frequently ensures only that yesterday's methods and standards are applied tolerably well. *A degree still provides too many graduates with a reasonable basis for living in the recent past.*

Reluctance to Innovate

The reluctance to innovate is partly ideological. A paper which I read in 1988 to the British Association for the Advancement of Science met with a vigorous response from academics because I argued that 'much of the academic community . . . seems to have contracted out of Mrs Thatcher's Britain'.[1] I made this claim because, having been Chairman of the Economic and Social Research Council (ESRC) from 1983 to 1987, I had more opportunity than most to observe research by academics in British universities. For example, I found it astonishing that, as late as 1985, a group of eminent social scientists at an ESRC meeting argued that what happened in Britain in the 1980s was simply an aberration caused by Mrs Thatcher and that once a non-Conservative government was elected the familiar land-scape of the 1960s or 1970s would re-emerge. This may not, even then, have been a general view but the fact that it could be held by an élite group as strongly as it was in 1985, shows how effectively, behind their interlocking monopolies, the univer-sities had retreated into their bunker.

Besides being ideological, the bunker is intellectual. Again, when I came to the ESRC in 1983 I found it odd, to say the least, that most of the research it financed and presumably most of the researchers were somehow stuck in the 1960s, despite the dramatic technological and other changes resulting from devel-opments in information technology and high technology—to say nothing of the emergence of the knowledge industries. I

[1] Douglas Hague, 'Establishing Research Priorities in the Social Sciences', in Phyllis Deane, *Frontiers of Economic Research*, Basingstoke and London: Macmillan, 1990, especially pp. 32-33.

presumed that this failing was confined to social scientists, though I found it strange that the only group whose profession was specifically concerned with economic and social analysis should be so unwilling to keep themselves up to date. I was therefore in one sense relieved—but in another disappointed—when assured in 1985 by an eminent physical scientist, closely concerned with evaluating the national research effort in the natural sciences, that the same criticism would be equally true of natural scientists—that far too many were still stranded in the 1960s.

Part of the problem is specialisation. Buttressed in their academic bunker, its denizens do not seek to become polymaths, who are now an endangered species. Instead, they presume greater mastery of limited fields, perhaps never recalling the old saw about knowing everything about nothing. Peter Hennessy, in an unpublished lecture, refers to hyper-specialism as always a British problem but

'now a blight at pretty well every level. And specialism is not synonymous with excellence. It produces books that do not travel, teachers whose words do not sing and a political nation deficient in the wherewithal for understanding and rational debate.

'It's an example of deformation that leaves professionals unable to talk to each other, ever prone to caricature and dismissing what they don't understand. To create a grand corps of educators up to the wider task ... something will have to be done about that.'[1]

Not only does this mean that the broad wisdom of the polymath—which universities so badly need—is confined to too few heads. It is also one reason why too much academic research is out of date, stuck with outdated paradigms. All too quickly new paradigms become outmoded. But intellectual establishments age as their paradigms age; innovations are kept out. Especially in a university system which has ceased to grow much, and where academic posts give life-long tenure, intellectual atrophy all too easily sets in. The system and its sub-systems become impermeable.

There is lack of innovation also in the way universities are organised. We shall see that pressure from the University Grants Committee, now succeeded by the Universities Funding Council (UFC) has, among other things, forced universities even to tiptoe

1 Peter Hennessy, unpublished lecture to an Educational Innovation Conference, Templeton College, Oxford, July 1990.

towards corporate planning. Most universities do this grudgingly and therefore obtain minimum benefit from what should be a stimulating experience, while the UFC has too little first-rate management expertise to be able to help this along significantly, even if it wanted to do so. Nor is there much interest in improved management among academics, though there is more—often much more—among university administrators. Innovation, flexibility and above all rapid response remain too rare in universities, especially in teaching and research.

In consultancy, the position is different. Those who do not change do not have enough external clients; those who do are prepared to change because clients insist on it. In research, quite apart from the fact that 'counting' research publications is not the best way to assess a university's research performance, to the extent that the quality *is* assessed that assessment is by the individual's own over-specialised, inward-looking peer group.

The UGC/UFC's Reforms: More Students and Competition . . .

At this point, we must examine in more detail the changes initiated by the UGC and UFC since the middle 1980s. I shall deal here with the two most important.

First, the UFC has recently sought to push universities to accept increasing numbers of students so that more than the current percentage of the appropriate age group in the UK receives university education. This might have been more acceptable to the universities, had the UFC not insisted on achieving it at a lower cost per student.

There have been two stages. In 1988, the UGC changed its arrangements for financing universities, linking their income to numbers of students, but increasing total government grants to universities by less than the increase in student numbers. Indeed, between 1989 and 1990, the number of students increased by about 13 per cent but there was no increase (in real terms) in the amount of money the UFC paid for their training.

In 1990, the UFC sought to introduce a degree of competition through what was effectively a simulated market. Under what *The Economist* has described as 'a fiendishly complicated bidding system',[1] the UFC attempted to induce universities to reduce further the average cost per student. To assist them with their bids for students, the UFC published guide prices, but made it clear that only those universities offering to educate

[1] *The Economist*, 10 November 1990, p. 30.

students for *less* than the guide prices would be granted extra funds.

In the event, the universities rebelled, offering only 7 per cent of their places at below the guide price. What is not clear is whether their rebellion took the form of tacit or of overt agreements to bid only at the guide price, the universities have 'denied that they had sabotaged the system by forming a cartel'.[1]

In February 1991, the UFC announced that the universities had put in bids for government finance for 335,000 UK students, which was close to the target figure previously published by the Government. In the event, the UFC had decided to finance only 304,000 students. In addition, however, the UFC expected that the universities would wish to take in further students without a government grant, charging them only the normal student fee. Indeed, it was reported[2] that, from 1992, the UFC would force universities to take on yet more students on this 'fees only' basis as an incentive to win more fully-funded places. Fees-only payments cover only about half of a university's estimated cost per student.

The UGC therefore estimate that in 1991/92 there will be an increase of 7 per cent in numbers of university students, against 17 per cent in polytechnics and colleges of higher education. This would give a total of about 380,000 university students in 1991/92, three-quarters of them undergraduates.

Some of these institutions, especially University College, London and the London School of Economics, have begun to talk of requiring students themselves to pay a smallish extra fee, so that this is very much a continuing saga.

. . . and Pressure to Improve Research

The second way in which the UGC/UFC have put pressure on universities is through two 'research selectivity exercises', in 1986 and 1989. These are concerned with research because, as readers will appreciate, apart from funding students on the lines just discussed, the UFC (and UGC before it) pays a substantial amount to each university which covers that part of their academics' time which is, notionally at least, devoted to research. As the UGC had in 1986, the UFC called in 1989 for a large amount of information, especially about university academics and about research. The aim was to supplement the pressure towards training more students at lower average costs

[1] *The Independent*, 3 April 1991, p. 2.   [2] *The Times*, 26 February 1991, p. 4.

with a similar pressure to increase the quality of research and of its management in universities.

For each member of the academic staff, the UFC sought information not only about their professional position but about publications, 'other publicly identifiable output'; success in obtaining research grants, studentships, and research contracts; and a professional assessment of the performance of each by a panel whose general approach would, according to a UFC circular, 'be that of an informed peer group review'.

To check on research by individuals, the UFC asked for the total number of books, parts of books and articles in academic journals written by each—a clear case of counting quantity rather than assessing quality. In addition, however, the council asked each university, for each academic, to list up to two publications, indicating any of these which were 'of major significance'.

For the university or college as a whole, or large research units within it, the UFC sought information about the institution's research plans and objectives; their success in monitoring these; the way in which research was managed, and so on.

The Impact of the Reforms

The UFC has used the information obtained from this survey—and discussions with academics from each university—to determine the size of that part of the university's grant intended to finance research. The amount was increased or maintained for 'good' (my inverted commas) universities and reduced for others.

In thumbnail sketches of the results of the selectivity exercise, the UFC has given examples of what has been achieved. Thus, for example, a medium-sized civic university had reduced the range of its academic activities, closed departments and re-directed research, while showing selectivity in making staff reductions. It had formed new departments and their research objectives had been identified. New processes for planning and resource allocation had been established, with a new committee to oversee research activities. The UFC saw this as 'a major exercise in selectivity' and, by implication at least, one to be commended.

I readily accept that the UGC/UFC moves to reduce costs per student in teaching and to concentrate research in universities and departments which have good research results has led to substantial changes in what universities do and how they do it.

More young people are being given a university education at a lower average cost than before. Universities are taking the planning and management of their research more seriously than ever.

It is too early to judge what impact the UFC's insistence that the universities should take in more students will have on the calibre and training of graduates. What *is* clear is that more selectivity in recruiting or retaining academic staff and in the research they carry out—either as individuals or units—is leading all universities to think much more carefully about the nature and quality of their research. I do, however, have two worries.

First, academic research is now being judged almost entirely by academics alone, on criteria which are probably not appropriate in the knowledge society. Second, and much more important, the whole research selectivity exercise requires universities to answer large numbers of detailed questions. Funds are then being allocated in the belief that bureaucrats and academics at the centre can best make that allocation. I would worry about such a procedure at any time, because it means that conventional academic and bureaucratic wisdom would prevail. I worry more about it at a time when the development of the knowledge industries and of information technology is leading to dramatic changes in the relative importance and rôles of universities and of knowledge businesses. Worst of all, I worry because having academics and bureaucrats in London sitting in judgement on them from above must be the best recipe for demoralising the universities. Even if those judgements are correct, the very making of the judgements implies that universities are trusted neither to carry out appropriate and high-quality research nor to manage it well.

Corporate Planning the Best Solution

I sympathise with this view, but not with the solution adopted. It would be infinitely preferable to work through good corporate planning. If centralised control is to continue, then each university should be asked to agree its corporate plan with the UFC and, in particular, to agree the objectives which it is to pursue. Those objectives would *have* to be worked out by the university and not imposed by the centre. After this, far from being asked questions by others, each university would be made to ask *itself* questions at appropriate intervals, to ensure that the plan and its objectives were being met. The UFC would then have to be convinced by the university that the latter was meeting *its own* agreed objectives and hence the agreed plan. This would motivate the universities much more successfully, and do so with less effort. It would also end the worst feature of the selectivity exercise which is that it seeks to force all universities into a similar mould.

Relying on corporate plans would be an improvement on present arrangements, but I shall suggest what I believe to be an even better solution in Section VII.

A final point must be made here. Currently, those in universities worry about their collective morale. Both most insiders and many outsiders blame its low state on low salaries and lack of funds generally. There are, however, more fundamental reasons why so many academics are currently so miserable. First, universities have ceased to be the power-houses they have been, in large part because of the passage of time. One reason for this is that the implicit *raison d'être* of universities is, by training new brains, to destroy their own monopoly of brain-power. University graduates, translated to knowledge businesses, and to knowledge jobs in other businesses, are emerging as powerful competitors to those who trained them.

Perhaps, there is an even deeper reason for low morale, especially in the more privileged colleges and universities, where academics have time, leisure and libraries which enable them to pursue their private intellectual passions. What more can they ask? Success is fine, but if what they do does not bring the results or recognition they expect, they become embittered. They are the last gilded manifestation of Thorsten Veblen's leisure class, 'illogical survivals', in Ernest Gellner's words, 'from a pre-industrial, predatory age', exemplifying 'the frills and affectations attached to higher education'.[1]

Summary

To sum up, this section shows that British universities represent a sheltered system, shielded from competitive pressure by two types of monopoly: natural monopolies of brain-power and of certain physical resources, like libraries or laboratories; and man-made monopolies, bestowed by government, first, through restrictions on the power to confer degrees and, second, through the university cartel.

Over time, the growth of the knowledge industries will give

[1] Ernest Gellner, *Nations and Nationalism*, Oxford: Blackwell, 1983, p. 27.

organisations outside the universities the potential to erode these monopolies. The extent to which and the speed with which this happens will, however, depend partly on what governments do. We return to that question in Section VII.

(d) Some Theory

So far, though, we have concentrated on facts. The position of the universities can, however, be put into a broader context, which leads to a dramatic conclusion. The context I find most illuminating is in *Nations and Nationalism* by the distinguished Cambridge anthropologist, Ernest Gellner[1]—an altogether engrossing book. It appears to be about nationalism—indeed, it *is* about nationalism—but it also contains a challenging analysis of the rôle of education in an industrial society.

Gellner's argument is that only with the development of industrial society was the ideal of continuous improvement 'invented', though this is not without its problems. For an industrial society:

> 'Its favourite method of social control is universal Danegeld, buying off social aggression with material enhancement; its greatest weakness is its inability to survive any temporary reduction of the social bribery fund, and to weather the loss of legitimacy which befalls it if this cornucopia becomes temporarily jammed and the flow falters.'[2]

Gellner goes on to argue that the steadily growing productivity which alone can guarantee economic progress requires not only a complex and refined division of labour, but 'an unstable, rapidly changing' one.[3] A successful industrial society 'is thereby committed to the need for innovation and hence to a changing occupational structure'.[4] As a result, certainly between generations and very often within single life-spans, people must be ready for re-allocation to new tasks.

Generic Education in the Information Society

Such a society has a number of typical characteristics, not least the development of growing specialisation. Each of the functions carried out in that society has 'at least one kind of specialist associated with it'.[5] What may appear to be paradoxical, but is not, is that training for such specialised tasks must be *preceded* by a generic training for every young person, which 'is unquestionably the *least* specialised, the most universally

---

[1] See previous footnote on page 31.   [2] *Ibid.*, p. 22.

[3] *Ibid.*, p. 32   [4] *Ibid.*   [5] *Ibid.*, p. 26.

standardised, that has ever existed'.[1] Gellner goes on to explain what happens once the generic training has been completed:

'Generally speaking the additional skills required consist of a few techniques that can be learned fairly quickly, plus "experience", a kind of familiarity with a milieu, its personnel and its manner of operation.'[2]

The second distinguishing feature of the industrial society is that, for an increasing proportion of those who work in it, jobs primarily require them to give and receive information, whether to and from other people or through understanding and responding to signals from machines or computers. They need, in Gellner's words, 'some standard idiom intelligible to all comers'.[3] That is what *generic* education has to provide. Gellner argues that this is true at *all* (but does he include even the earliest?) stages of industrialisation. It is certainly true when the knowledge industries play as large a part in the economy as they do today.

Gellner's thesis links to many parts of the argument in this *Paper* but is perhaps most helpful in throwing light on what I have called the university's monopoly of brain-power. He points out that those who run the educational system in a society like ours, through their *own* activities, guarantee that they no longer have 'monopoly of access to the written word'[4] which they had in an extreme form before and immediately after the invention of the printing press and have had to a diminishing degree since then. They work to destroy their own monopolies. A crucial corollary for our own argument is that, since the clientele of the educational system

'is co-extensive with the society at large ... the replaceability of individuals within the system by others applies to the educational machine at least as much as to any segment of society, and perhaps more so. Some very great teachers and researchers may perhaps be unique and irreplaceable, but the average professor ... can be replaced from outside the teaching profession with the greatest of ease and often with little, if any, loss'.[5]

This final point is important, and we return to it in Section VI.

---

[1] *Ibid.*, p. 27.   [2] *Ibid.*, p. 28.   [3] *Ibid.*, p. 33.
[4] *Ibid.*, p. 35.   [5] *Ibid.*, pp. 35-36.

IV. THE KNOWLEDGE INDUSTRIES

The knowledge industries encompass activities like research and development, design, information technology (especially writing computer software), consultancy, training, financial advice or management, including the management of pension funds or of personal savings. Their common characteristics are: that they require clever people; that they use relatively small amounts of capital equipment; and that they are organised very flexibly with a significant proportion of their people working, for at least part of their time, from home.

Many who work in the knowledge industries we are concentrating on are graduates, from a wide range of disciplines. They are highly motivated, hard working and determined to be true professionals, keeping their expertise up to date through learning on the job or through internal or external training courses. There are, therefore, smaller differences in education and levels of skill than in more traditional businesses, while their training will—or *should*—emphasise the need for lateral and original thinking. They are mainly youngish people, partly because a fair proportion of today's professional skills— especially in programming and using computers—are most frequently found and most up-to-date among the young. This will largely perpetuate itself, because most 40-year-olds—not to say 50- or 60-year-olds—feel out of place in such a milieu. Partly for this reason, hierarchies are less important. Christian names are always used; knowledge is pooled; few instructions are given. Yet, as in universities, individuals will want to be given greater credit for their own contribution to the organisation—especially its thinking—and ways of permitting this will have to be found.

Because we are concerned with the relationships between *universities* and the knowledge industries, this section will consider the knowledge businesses which seem most competitive with the universities, namely, information technology, consultancy and training.

The youngsters in these knowledge industries will often be at least as clever as their counterparts in universities, though it remains to be seen how many will still stand the pace of these

[34]

new organisations when they as individuals reach middle age. The organisations have not yet lasted long enough for us to know. The most successful are archetypal 'yuppies', but economic principles apply even to them. They are paid as much as they are only because they are scarce. As time passes, and more of them appear, disparities of pay will narrow, even if they do not vanish. That will happen as the supply increases faster than demand, providing an adequate supply of young people with degrees. A good deal of the demand for qualified people will come from the knowledge industries—evidence of the complex web of both complementarity and competition between them and the universities.

The buildings of these knowledge industries are also unusual, often being less formal than stereotype offices; they are also less central to the job. As partners in any consultancy will tell you, the organisation is often happiest if there are no consultants in the office. Then they are with clients, earning their own and everyone else's keep. So there is no need to have so many individual offices, or even desks. Offices like this become rallying places for nomads. But with communications equipment—telephones and fax—they keep in touch. Such an organisation looks more than a little frivolous. But it works, and will increasingly become the norm, certainly in *these* knowledge industries and perhaps in most of them. Indeed, their informality—though not their energy level—is more like that of a university than of a major business.

What, then, is happening in the knowledge industries relevant to this *Paper*?

(a) Information Technology

In our context, information technology means computer software, computer programmes, etc. Information technology consultancy is seen as part of the field covered in sub-section (b) below, and computers themselves come from manufacturing businesses.

The number of computer software firms in the UK has grown fast in the last 30 years. Logica, a large organisation, was established about 30 years ago and a large number of other organisations, ranging from one-man businesses to a few companies as big as Logica itself, have since been established. The key assets of software companies are highly trained people. This is shown very strikingly by the fact that two-thirds of the shares in another large British company in this field—Hoskyns—were recently sold to a major French organisation at a price which valued Hoskyns as a whole at nearly £300 million. Yet, in its accounts for 1988, its net assets were shown as totalling only some £25 million. Much of the difference reflects the value to the company of the specialists who work in it.

Sales of software and related services in Europe are expected to double by 1994—to about £100 billion. In the UK, Logica has a turnover of about £120 million and Hoskyns one of about £180 million. This is a rapidly growing and diverse industry though, like most such industries, it is gradually becoming dominated by a smallish number of companies. Philip Swinstead, former Chairman of SD-Scicon, a Franco-British software company, has suggested that some three or four businesses will emerge from and dominate the fragmented European market in the next few years.

The important point, for us, is that the biggest organisations are large by comparison with most universities and that the UK software industry as a whole is bigger still. Indeed, the dominance of these big organisations may increase. *The Economist* has recently suggested that the smaller software companies are in danger of losing market share.

> 'Nibbling away at their market comes "packaged" software, mass-produced standardised programmes that plug in and run without much tweaking by clever consultants. Back in 1979 this sort of product took only 11 per cent of Europe's software and services market; by 1989 the share had grown to 29 per cent.'[1]

As this happens, the specialist software companies will 'have to find even niftier things to offer'.[2] This will require them to put a bigger emphasis on personal service, that is, on consultancy, and may well bring them more into competition with general consultants, to whom we now turn.

(b) Consultancy

This is the broadest possible knowledge industry, because consultants can provide help to every kind of organisation and in every specialist field. No-one knows the exact number of consultancy companies in the UK, but it is clearly large and has grown rapidly during the 1980s. An important development in

---

[1] *The Economist*, 11 August 1990, p. 67.

[2] *Ibid.*

that decade was the establishment of consultancy arms by the big accountancy firms which did not already have them, and rapid growth in all of them. Most of these consultancy arms are now large, in some cases bigger than the auditing businesses from which they sprang. All offer consultancy over a much wider field than the financial area in which they began.

While there are many large consultancy companies covering virtually every field, there are also enormous numbers of small ones. One of the difficulties in discovering the precise size of the consultancy industry goes back to the issue addressed in Section II of this *Paper*. Our British obsession with the primacy of manufacturing means that official statistics relating to consultancy—and, indeed, other knowledge businesses—are less adequate than they should be.

Many consultancies are archetypal businesses of the kind described earlier in this section: employing large numbers of people, many of them at least as well trained and clever as most academics; using relatively few capital assets—mainly buildings and computers; and very flexible and informal in the ways they operate.

Since consultancy companies usually work for other—often bigger—companies they are typical of the 'contractual fringe'. Their *raison d'être* is to improve the performance and profitability of Britain's businesses and other organisations—not least the biggest—in both the public and private sectors; and they earn substantial amounts of foreign currency from working overseas.

One must, of course, add that some large industrial and commercial concerns have their own consultancy operations which may engage in work for other organisations as well as the parent firm. This adds to the complexity of the knowledge industries but does not alter their nature.

(c) Training

Training is a field where the size of the 'contractual fringe' has recently grown significantly, with a great deal of training provided by businesses, large and small, in the knowledge industries. Only a few of these organisations could, in principle, carry out university-level work and most of that would have to be professional development in fields like engineering or management rather than education in the strict sense.

Where businesses provide high-level training for their own employees there are two disadvantages. First, what they provide is often expensive, especially for senior managers. Salaries, pensions and related costs are relatively high for those who train senior managers, and operating a company's own—often rather luxurious—training centre is expensive too, unless large numbers of people attend the centre when at least the unit cost is brought down. It is, however, unlikely that large numbers of senior managers *will* attend, simply because only very large organisations will have many of them. This puts the contractual fringe, which frequently operates by hiring training facilities as necessary, at an advantage.

The second disadvantage of in-company training organisations is that they are somewhat inflexible. If a particular programme is ended it may not be easy to switch training staff to other activities. If an outside organisation is used instead, courses can be discontinued at relatively short notice, the onus then being on the contractor to find new work for his staff. This will also be easier for the contractor because he will normally work for a number of organisations so that finding new work as old work comes to an end is part of his way of life. Another part of that way of life may be running 'public' courses for employees of a number of organisations. He then has a problem only if the public programme ceases to attract sufficient participants to make it a commercial success.

In high-level management training, there are a number of substantial, well-established colleges, for example, at Henley and Ashridge. Where these are engaged in non-degree work there is no constraint on their activities except for the normal commercial ones of profit and loss, so that many of their courses compete directly with those in university business schools. Because the power to award degrees is jealously guarded, most cannot at present do so. Henley is unusual because it has established links with Brunel University, which enable it to offer MBA degrees. It is therefore an example—if a relatively small one—of permeability in the university system.

In addition to these institutions which are big—at least by the standards of this 'industry'—a very large number of small organisations offer programmes of their own, often drawing for lecturers and tutors on businesses or on university and business school academics. They rent accommodation in hotels or training centres—sometimes in universities. Indeed, many of those in charge of these small organisations either still are, or have been, university teachers themselves who operate successfully in a penumbral zone between the private business and the university.

It is impossible to give a figure for the aggregate turnover of these organisations. There was a boom in high-level management training in the late 1980s, some of which represented a cyclical upswing reflecting high company profits; but there has also been a growing and widespread recognition of the necessity for training as the knowledge society develops. The trend too must be upward.

(d) The Freelance Fringe

My use of the word 'penumbra' makes clear that there is no sharp dividing line between the knowledge industries and the universities. Just as an increasing number of organisations and individuals form the 'contractual fringe' round businesses, public and private, there is also a fringe (contractual or not) round the universities. Most of *this* fringe is made up of individuals rather than organisations though, from a strictly legal point of view, a significant proportion of them have set themselves up as companies.

Many who work in the contractual fringe round universities were previously employed by them. Some took early retirement during the period when universities were encouraged to grant it to older employees, in order to be able to offer more jobs to younger people, thereby maintaining a better spread of ages in the university. Some then saw advantages in staying close to the universities because they did not want to lose contact with them and found it convenient to do a certain amount of work—including part-time teaching—for them.

Younger members of the freelance fringe had more positive reasons for joining it. They continue as part of the fringe for a variety of reasons, but among them is the wish: to be able to change what they are doing and how they are doing it without having to wait for the ponderous academic and administrative machinery of a university to change too; to be free from university pay arrangements; to be flexible; and, above all, to be free to work and to innovate in their own way. Being able to pick and choose in what they do, they can innovate where they wish and work as and where they like.

This by no means implies that innovation is concerned only with the *processes* of organisations. An important minority of this contractual fringe seeks innovation in thinking and analysis.

[39]

They are based outside universities because they find academics in universities resistant to the ideas they seek to introduce or too set in their ways to be genuinely creative. There are now enough lively thinkers outside the universities to make it easy for such people to stimulate each others' thought, where it was not a decade ago.

Innovation in university teaching, in research and in the working of their organisations themselves is vital. Yet it is often only those on the fringes of universities who have enough freedom to carry out experiments which universities can then copy. Universities need to keep in close contact with the freelance fringe as well as with knowledge businesses.

I do not imply that because members of the freelance fringe have their roots more in universities than in business, their contacts with business and their understanding of its methods is weak. Especially in professional subjects, they bring a commercial ethic and an understanding of commercial practices which the modern university desperately needs. One of the most encouraging aspects of the information underlying this *Paper* is the clear indication that the number of younger members of this intellectual penumbra is increasing. As the knowledge society develops, this is bringing the hope that their vitality and enthusiasm will exert a growing influence on society as a whole and on the universities in particular.

V. THE KNOWLEDGE REVOLUTION AND THE UNIVERSITIES: INTERACTIONS

I begin this section by looking at some predictions. Futurologists face two main difficulties. They may point to trends which seem important but which lead nowhere. Or they may pick out the right trends but get their timing wrong. When he wrote *Future Shock*, in 1970, Alvin Toffler had a great deal to say about education. The rate of change in this field has been slower than he predicted, but I believe that events will prove him correct in having identified the broad direction in which education will move.

In particular, Toffler pointed out that in the technological society of the future, machines would handle physical movements, while men would handle 'the flow of information and insight'.[1] He also predicted that human work would move from the factory and large office to the locality and the home. That too is happening, though still slowly.

As these developments take place, 'the most valued attributes of the individual even become handicaps'.[2] The knowledge society requires people who can reach good decisions, cope with new environments, spot new rules—human and physical—as the world changes. The objective of education should therefore now be to inculcate what Toffler calls 'cope-ability', in a world where change is more rapid than ever.

Toffler therefore insisted, in 1970, that society must generate and debate alternative views of the technologies, the organisation structures, the jobs, the human relationships and the communal and business ethos of the future. We have not yet achieved this, though perhaps there is still time.

Toffler goes on to raise some questions at which I have hinted, though he does so more for schools than universities. In particular he asks: How will our educational organisations change? Should education take place in schools (we might say universities) at all? He advocates the dispersal and decentralisation of education and its inter-penetration with the community, because education must develop men and women who can cope

[1] Alvin Toffler, *Future Shock*, New York: Bantam Books, 1970, p. 402.
[2] *Ibid.*, p. 402.

[41]

happily with the future. We must therefore abandon one basic precept of industrial society. This was that we were training people 'to occupy a comparatively permanent slot in the social and economic order'.[1] Instead, we must 'prepare people to function in temporary organisations'[2]—like those of the knowledge society.

The rest of Toffler's book must be read for itself, but there is one argument which points, as it were like a searchlight, at British universities.

Diversity, not Standardisation

The key to the rapid industrialisation of North America and Western Europe before and after the Second World War was, of course, standardisation—whose most memorable slogan was Henry Ford's: 'Any colour so long as it's black'. Industrial techniques could only thrive, we believed, if based on the standardisation of skill, technique and product.

Toffler saw, back in 1970, that technological development now offers us diversity. Today's purchaser of a motor car can choose his 'own', instructing the seller's computer to give him the mixture of styles and accessories he chooses. Even in 1970, the purchaser of a Ford Mustang had well over 200 combinations to choose from, and that was before selecting its colour and original equipment. Technology is rapidly de-standardising the material world, and this leads Toffler to a dramatic vision.

Education in industrial countries, and not least in the USA, has offered what are effectively standard packages, certainly within the school or classroom. In the knowledge society this will be neither necessary nor acceptable. There can be argument over the timing of this development, but I believe the central point is fundamental to my case.

> 'Long before the year 2000, the entire antiquated structure of degrees, majors and credits will be a shambles. No two students will move along exactly the same educational track. For the students now pressuring higher education to de-standardise, to move towards super-industrial diversity, will win their battle.'[3]

Because the educational system of the American city has its full share of the entrenched interests and prejudices also found in the British university, Toffler questioned how soon this might happen in a city like New York. But he again foreshadowed the

---

[1] *Ibid.*, p. 408.   [2] *Ibid.*   [3] *Ibid.*, p. 273.

argument in this *Paper*. 'Failure to diversify education *within* the system will simply lead to the growth of alternative educational opportunities *outside* the system',[1] he claimed.

(a) Education and Training

Against this background, I now consider the impact of the knowledge revolution on British universities. I shall begin, reversing the order in Section IV, with education and training, because this is the main rôle of a British university. It is also where developments in information and communications technology will have their biggest impact on universities in the next two decades.

In its main activity—preparing students studying for first degrees—the university provides three things: information, integration, and inter-action.

The *informative* rôle is obvious. Students obtain information from lectures, articles, books, etc., and, though I would argue strongly that it should not be so, *most* students obtain *most* of the information which their university education gives them from lectures. So much so, that I sometimes ask university colleagues how they expect to come to terms with what information technology has to offer when they have not yet come fully to terms with the invention of the printing press. And that is only partly a joke.

In many universities and colleges, too many lectures are still not well-enough prepared or delivered. Even if they were, the rôle of an economist is to remind his audience of the importance of the division of labour. For example, in every week of the university term, several hundred lectures in (say) first-year economics are delivered in the UK. Some, I know, are given by well-prepared lecturers, who deserve and get large audiences. Many are not. But that is not the point. It will soon be possible for the good—even the best—lectures to be replaced by televised or video-taped presentations by world authorities. Lectures will increasingly become available in both formats and will be increasingly cheap. Moreover, animated diagrams and graphs— or clippings from films—will be included. It is vital that the new technology does what it is good at, and that is not simply to reproduce what is traditional—the lecture. Academics can then concentrate on running tutorials or advising students.

Nor is this all. A cult literature now prized in Cambridge,

[1] *Ibid.*, p. 294.

[43]

England, is scribbled notes from Keynes's lectures and discussions. What would we not give now (what would we not have given then?) to be able to look in on discussions between Keynes, Dennis Robertson, Richard Kahn, and Joan and Austin Robinson? And the same was true for Milton Friedman and his associates. Pathé News could not have got into Keynes's room in the 1930s. With smaller, modern cameras and sound recorders, we *can* now eavesdrop on the great—though as yet few publishers and very few universities have had the gumption to do so.

This is what is required. Not *only* the formal lecture or TV programme but all undergraduates sitting in their rooms listening to great men and women thinking aloud. Otherwise we never get a real impression of the *man*—or *woman*. The world's best brain-power captured in this way will dramatically increase the rate of circulation of intellectual capital.

Those to whom I have put some of the ideas in this *Paper* take a lofty view of all this. They respond: *This* did not happen when I read economics at Cambridge, Oxford or the LSE. Maybe not. But that, again, is not the point. *Most* university students do *not* read economics—or indeed anything else—in Oxbridge or London. Nor, I may add, do students of non-university colleges in Britain—let alone students overseas.

Pressure to Maximise Economies of Scale

In the knowledge society, the pressure to achieve economies of scale on the part of those who will make films or videos and of those who will provide educational television will merge with the need to educate as many as possible to as high a level as they can attain. That is true whether or not, before the knowledge society arrived, this would have been the case. We are no longer concerned with how to educate an élite, or even with education in a single country.

We must return here to Toffler's point about standardisation and choice because, whenever it is put to academics, they respond that most people prefer old-fashioned ways. Very well— *if* that is what they *really* want and *if* students or the state will pay appropriately high fees. Students may not. They may still prefer the comradeship of a lecture hall but yet prefer a presentation by a world authority. Others may prefer to watch television or video tapes at times and places of their own choosing. Some may prefer to continue to use books instead: that, too, is their right.

[44]

We must, however, grasp what the processes of information technology will offer educationalists who seek to *integrate* knowledge. Before long, it will be possible to link computers, television screens, video and audio tapes and large databases. The student will be able not merely to question and respond to the computer, but also to watch appropriate clips from films, to listen to appropriate tapes, or to read selected passages from the television screen.

A whole world of choice is opening up and, given the possibility of choice, we must allow even students to choose. To the rôle of the tutor will be added that of an educational manager or, as I prefer, 'educational consultant' helping each student to work out an appropriate programme for him/herself, as well as giving him or her the opportunity for face-to-face discussion.

Of course, no such system is yet complete, but we should begin to move in this direction, even while incomplete choice is available.

Again, I quote Peter Hennessy:

'If half the ingenuity of what we put into television advertising went into the media side of educational experience, we would be on our way. Who wouldn't rather have their European history from the mouth of an A. J. P. Taylor than from your struggling, over-stretched, over-familiar teacher at the textbook face?'[1]

He adds rightly, however, that this is not to diminish the need for the latter, or to omit praise for him.

At this point the patience of the academic usually breaks down. 'What you don't realise', he insists, 'is that university education is far more than disembodied learning—achieved by communing with a computer. The key rôle of the university lies in *interaction*; the most important element is interaction with tutors and fellow students in seminars, tutorials and social activity. A university which relies on information technology will lack the ingredient which has made university education what it is. Education by information technology cannot offer interaction, and so is doomed. Traditional university education is safe.'

We must now isolate and discuss the issues which this response raises.

---

[1] Peter Hennessy (1990), *op. cit.*

(i) Using Technology to Create Time for Productive Interaction
First, we can take the argument on its own terms. Interaction
with tutors and in seminars, and so on, clearly *is* an important
part of the educational process in a university, but getting the
best value out of information and communication technology
does not mean the demise of tutors or of seminars. I have
already argued that with first-rate programmes available via
television or video-tape, more time of more academics will be
released for individual and group discussions, some of them
relating back to the televised material. More time will be
available for precisely the kind of activity the critics prize, quite
apart from the fact that when the student works with an
interactive system he or she is not communing with a computer,
but with knowledge.

To take the line that interaction is impossible in a degree
programme which uses television is also, of course, to insult the
Open University which currently has some 11,000 part-time
first-degree students. It has for years pioneered courses which
give students working from home an opportunity for interaction
in local tutorial groups. Moreover, Open University students
have the privilege—not offered in the traditional university—of
working with tutors from public- and private-sector organisations who are as eminent as John Bourn, Comptroller and
Auditor General of the UK. There are also well-established and
very successful Open University Summer Schools.

If the number of part-time degree students seems small, the
total number of Open University students, at about 180,000, is
large. Many of these are taking a part of a degree-level course
and therefore may register for a degree later. The total also
includes 80,000 'clients', as the University calls them, who are
studying courses out of interest and will not take formal
examinations. *There* is the diversity and scale which I expect to
see in 21st-century universities.

Even to discuss the Open University, however, is too much to
force the developments made possible by information technology into the mould of the traditional university. My point is
that, for the first time, information technology will allow us to
break this mould. An inkling of what is possible appears when,
having for a time left my writing at the end of the last paragraph,
and turning on the television set, by coincidence I see the Vice-
Chancellor of the Open University extolling the benefits being
derived from the home-computer programme which his Univer-

sity has recently launched. He does so more convincingly because he is 'there' in my sitting-room. This is the power of the media—immediacy at the touch of a switch, *wherever* we choose to be and *whenever* and *whatever* we choose to watch.

The home computing course itself is 'extremely popular' and there are currently eight courses aimed at teaching basic computer literacy. These have been devised to improve competence either as a student or an employee; to provide another way of presenting teaching material; to give a network through which Open University students, staff and tutors can communicate, and so on. Nearly 15,000 students registered for these courses in 1990. Most have access to their own personal computers but about 3,000 are renting machines under a scheme established by the Open University, with government support.

As another example, students on the part-time MBA programme of the Cranfield Institute of Technology are taking part in an experiment which is seeking to break the mould. In 1989, the Cranfield Management School *gave* each member of this programme a personal computer, together with free telephone time. This has enabled every member of the programme to communicate with any or all of the others at will by electronic mail and free of charge—in the periods between residential sessions at Cranfield.

Video and Audio Conferencing

At present, communication via computer or facsimile machine is the limit of innovation in most universities. We have seen that it will not be long before video-conferencing will also be relatively cheap so that modest-sized groups of people (or indeed individuals) will communicate in this way, with television pictures of whoever is speaking shown to everyone. This will soon be possible over telephone lines which are upgraded little, if at all, above what is currently normal and with capital equipment whose price will fall dramatically during the 1990s.

We should not exaggerate the speed at which such technical developments will take place but, once they have, we shall soon adapt ourselves to using them. Those who around 1960 allowed themselves to be convinced that developments in computers and computing would transform the world within a decade were disappointed by the lack of progress in the 1960s and 1970s; in the 1980s, the advances were dramatic. It would be rash to dismiss the developments foreshadowed here as science fiction. They are not.

[47]

Nor should we be too insular. If we live in the UK, or another small Western European country, internal distances are short and even part-time students can reach a university or tutorial centre relatively easily. Our attitude to what information technology will make possible would be very different were we concerned with education in the more sparsely populated parts of the USA, Canada, Australia, the USSR or China. Some universities in North America are now linked by television to 'satellite' sites up to 600 miles away—the distance from London almost to Prague—with easy conversation between centre and periphery. Education for school children, university students and adults is being transformed.

To believe that the traditional UK university can remain immune to these developments is simply unrealistic. Yet that is what most academics ask us to do, at least so far as teaching is concerned. I shall argue later that we must make arrangements in the UK which ensure that barriers between the universities and knowledge industries are broken down, but we shall ignore developments overseas at our peril.

We must also remember an important parallel. Many who have argued for years about how best to regulate broadcasting within the UK now realise that satellite television has made this an international, not a domestic, issue. For example, the whole world has simultaneously watched reports on the Gulf War on CNN. Much of that earlier UK debate was wasted.

In the same way, the more universities in the UK turn their backs on what developments in information and communication technology make possible, the more they will face international competition. There is nothing to prevent distance-learning degrees being awarded by universities in Berlin, Harvard, Tokyo or Moscow. One is reminded of the famous remark by Joseph Schumpeter. In a modern economy, he argued, the kind of competition which really counts is

> 'from the new commodity, the new technology, the new source of supply, the new type of organisation ... competition which commands a decisive cost or quality advantage and which strikes not at the margins of the profits and outputs of the existing firms, but at their foundations and their very lives. This kind of competition is as much more effective than the other as a bombardment is in comparison with forcing a door'.[1]

[1] J. A. Schumpeter, *Capitalism, Socialism and Democracy*, London: Allen & Unwin, 1950, p. 84.

[48]

Of course, this exaggerates the impact of the information revolution on universities. They are not—not yet, at least—commercial businesses. But the basic issue is similar: Can the universities meet the challenge of technological change and of competition from knowledge industries which are brimming with brains and aided by technological change? And of international competition? Given the inevitability of choice, what the customer—the student—does will be decisive. There will be a spectrum of views among students as to what they want, from the traditional to the *avant-garde*; there will be overseas competition; there will, sooner or later, be competition from the private sector. Some students will doubtless continue to attend universities which cling to traditional ways of doing things, despite the fact that as salary levels rise with economic development they will become increasingly expensive. Others will not. Students will do what they want to do.

(ii) Degrees Tailored to Students' Requirements

Developments in information and communication technology will also make it less necessary than ever to obtain one's degree in the traditional three (or four) consecutive years, beginning at about 18 years of age. It will be possible, and one hopes encouraged, to study at an age, over a period and with a time pattern which suits the student, not the university. I am delighted that many universities, by introducing degrees made up of smallish 'modules', have taken their first steps towards this end. The ability to choose one's own timing will be as much a part of the ending of standardisation in education as will the ability to choose one's own mix of subjects and learning methods. Beyond that, in the knowledge society *lifetime* learning will have to be the norm. Only in that way can knowledge be kept abreast of what is needed in a changing world where knowledge itself will depreciate along with other capital assets.

In that world none of us should insist on prescribing what is proper behaviour—including the age at which we should learn. We must *not* replace what degree of control universities currently have over students with intellectual nannying, especially as the average age of students rises. Adult discussion with tutors, educational consultants and with parents, employers and friends must settle the pattern of the individual's education.

We who think in these ways are in a great tradition. Imagine R. H. Tawney who, as A. J. P. Taylor recounts, 'provided most of the moral inspiration' for the reforms instituted by the Board of Education in the early 1920s.

'Here was a great achievement, at any rate in principle; a clear recognition, again imperceptibly accepted by men of all parties, that the entire population, and not merely a privileged minority, were entitled to some education beyond "the three Rs".'[1]

Tawney would at once have seen what modern technology could offer and would have sought to use it.

The knowledge industries have so far had little impact on academics. Even the Open University, though a successful innovator in its own terms, has not yet achieved dramatic innovation. How, when and where dramatic innovations will come, and what rôle the knowledge industries will play in them, remains to be seen. But come they will.

(b) Research

(i) Science

This section is concerned mainly with basic research, but since that represents simply one end of a substantial spectrum, we shall look more widely afield too.

Given the agitation in the UK by scientists who claim that support for scientific research in general—and university scientific research in particular—is too small, policy-making would be much simplified if there were ways of showing clearly what the return to expenditure on basic science is. In a paper to the British Association for the Advancement of Science in 1989, Professor Keith Pavitt, of the Science Policy Research Unit at the University of Sussex, points out[2] that, in a complex world, there is no simple answer to what may, at first sight, appear a simple question. Professor Pavitt quotes Professor Paul David and his colleages at the Centre for Economic Policy Research at the University of Stanford, in California. They take the view, first, that the economic value of outputs from basic scientific research does not lie in any intrinsic feature of that research, but in the fact that a set of research results is an input to further research (and further results) and/or to industrial innovation. It is these *complementarities* which are crucial, so that policy-making should not focus exclusively on supporting basic research, but on the linkages identified here.

[1] A. J. P. Taylor, *English History, 1914-1945*, Pelican Books, Penguin, 1970, pp. 272-73.

[2] Keith Pavitt, 'What Do We Learn About the Usefulness of Science? The Case for Diversity', in Douglas Hague (ed.), *The Management of Science*, Basingstoke and London: Macmillan, 1991, p. 30.

Paul David and his colleagues go on to argue that we should regard basic research as a process of learning about the physical world that can better influence the process of applied research and development. Basic research does not lead to marketable products: rather it 'interacts with applied research in a complex and iterative manner to increase the productivity of both basic and applied research'.[1] We are back to permeability—to the importance of developing links between universities and private-sector research organisations, whether laboratories or businesses. We need greater contact between scientific researchers in universities and businesses which may be able to use basic research findings. In the UK, there has been increasing pressure in this direction through government-funded programmes like 'Link' and 'Alvey',[2] pressure which itself accepts that there has been too little interaction in the past.

Professor Pavitt also argues strongly that an important rôle of academic research is to produce trained researchers who, when they

'go on to work in applied activities . . . take with them not just the knowledge resulting from their research, but also skills, methods and a web of professional contacts that will help them tackle the technological problems they later face'.[3]

The more permeable universities become, the larger that web of contacts will be. That is another reason for my emphasis on permeability.

Interaction of Basic Research and Innovation

It is also important to recognise how complex is the way in which basic research and innovation interact. Professor Pavitt is unhappy that much of the pressure which government put on universities during the 1980s to become more engaged in research which *did* seem likely to have early application—what Whitehall jargon has christened 'strategic' research—was misguided. The evidence in its favour 'is ambiguous and incomplete'. He strongly believes that strategic research 'should be funded jointly by government and firms'.[4] I agree with him.

1 *Ibid.*, p. 30.

2 Both of these programmes were established to foster collaborative projects, and each was backed by government money. In the early 1980s, the 'Alvey' programme brought together one or more universities or polytechnics and one or more businesses—which provided up to half the finance—to conduct research into the applications of information technology. In the late 1980s, the 'Link' programme extended such collaboration into other new technologies, but was designed to avoid 'near-market' research.

3 *Ibid.*, p. 33.   4 *Ibid.*, p. 40.

What is more, I believe that it should be designed and, above all, *monitored* jointly through such alliances of talent.

I should add that as the 1980s ran their course, Whitehall itself accepted that the main direct rôle of government in this field was to finance basic research in universities.

The strengths of universities lie in basic rather than applied research, not in development—and perhaps not in application.

Businesses clearly welcome the opportunity of conversations with university researchers, which is one reason for the success of science parks associated with universities. The information and communications revolution will provide an opportunity to build on this. Science parks currently have to be physically close to universities because that is the only way to be close to researchers. Video-conferencing will change all of this because it will become possible to have discussions with experts around the country—and indeed the world—seeing as well as hearing them.

Here is an opportunity for universities to provide *distributed brain-power* to as widely-scattered a clientele as they wish. Making the most of such opportunities will not be without its problems, for example in determining how the individual academic shares any money that changes hands—a topic to which we return later in this section. Nevertheless, if the universities can work out ways to handle the provision of distributed brain-power, that will give them another major rôle in the knowledge society. The benefits both for them and for the nation will be substantial.

(ii) Social Science

To the extent that there *is* basic research in the social sciences, most is carried out in universities and covers the whole range of the social sciences. Some research is very good—not least in economics, economic history, psychology and some areas of geography. Even so, I have explained that when I was Chairman of the ESRC, my worry was that too much research was out of date. I was also worried because the average quality was lower than I was convinced it should have been.

In addition to this, two big failings of academic researchers—especially social scientists—are slowness in completing research and a lackadaisical approach to its dissemination. One gets the impression that most academics complete research so much in a state of exhaustion and/or boredom that they find it hard to ensure that its results reach those who should have them. They are assisted in this by book publishers who seem to share this unconcern about speedy publication and drive the academic who *is* concerned about it to despair. Until now there has been little that outsiders could do about slowness except complain; but the revolution in information and communications technology must surely change things. Natural scientists have traditionally made summaries of their findings available very quickly. Social scientists and others should do the same, and technology—with developments like 'desktop publishing'—will help them.

Although little basic research in the social sciences is carried out in private-sector institutions, private-sector bodies do finance research and seem to do so more effectively than does the public sector. When at the ESRC, I felt that private-sector organisations had two advantages. First, they seemed better at picking research winners. Second, their administrations were much more stream-lined. For example, the Leverhume Trust had a small staff and an efficient, computerised system. The ESRC did not. Despite my best efforts, the ESRC has still not totally shaken itself free from a highly bureaucratic and enormously labour-intensive system for assessing applications from researchers for support. The elaborateness and cost of this system result from two factors. First, a Utopian desire for 'fairness'. Second, a belief that only specialists in a field can judge other specialists in that field.

The Problem of 'Fairness'

The problem about attaining the unattainable over 'fairness' is probably insoluble since the passion for it seems to be part of the British disease leading, for example, to the complexity of the tax and social security systems. The belief that only experts can judge other experts has led to the peer review system, with its own defects. Certainly, the ethos of the universities has over-flowed into the ESRC, in the form of an infuriating belief that if only more and more people in appropriate academic disciplines spend more and more time evaluating longer and longer applications for support from members of those same disci-plines, then research grants will be allocated with precise fairness. Quite apart from the inherent unlikeliness that this will be the result, it was this system which missed the 'winners'.

If allowed, I would make the way in which the ESRC distributes research funds much more like that of Leverhume, but the ethos of the public sector would never tolerate it. As I said in 1984, in my Mond lecture at the University of Manchester, the problem in Whitehall is far too often that 'not only must what is done be fair; what is done must be seen to have been done in a way that ensures fairness; and that fairness must be demonstrable to ministers, to parliament and to the public. As a result, solutions to problems which I would regard as managerially efficient are ruled out because they imply, if you like, a degree of dictatorship'.[1]

I went on later to add:

'There is a permanent and inevitable tension in a democracy between managerial efficiency and constitutional propriety. It may be that, too often, we take constitutional propriety too seriously and so spend more than we need. This is certainly an issue which needs debate, but such debate will almost always end by requiring a more elaborate organisation than a purely "managerial" solution would. There is a price to be paid for Parliamentary accountability and democratic control. It is right that such a price should be paid. The important question is how much more we need to spend—to keep Parliament and the public happy—over and above what it would cost to achieve what a manager would regard as an efficient solution. For the price we currently pay—in money and in time "given" to public-sector work—is high.'[2]

Even when least aware that they are doing so, public-sector organisations always seem to be for job creation. Since alliances between the knowledge industry and the universities are likely to have least effect on basic research in the social sciences, I expect little improvement here.

Competition in Applied Research

In applied research the situation is very different—especially in applied economics. Many private-sector organisations work in this field, probably the biggest group being those which provide studies of the short-term position in the UK and other major economies. They have transformed the task of anyone keeping abreast of short-term economic developments, not least because most of the studies are produced by bankers and stockbroking companies in the City of London and are therefore available to businessmen, journalists, researchers, teachers and others, free of charge. Most of these reports are well-written and authoritative; some background papers reach an intellectual standard at least up to that of a university. More important, they are written on time and sometimes, as at Budget time, very quickly indeed. One could quibble over whether this is applied research or consultancy, though I prefer to see it as the former. The point is

[1] Douglas Hague, *Is Science Manageable?*, Mond Lecture, 1984, published by Manchester Literary and Philosophical Society (14 Kennedy Street, Manchester, M2 4BY), p. 15.
[2] *Ibid.*, p. 18.

that some of the most useful economic writing for businessmen, bankers, the media, even academics, does not come from the universities at all. The collective brain-power of those who write—Mr Lawson's 'teenage scribblers'—is powerful. The bodies close to universities which hold a strong position in macro-economic analysis and forecasting—like the London Business School or Oxford Economic Forecasting—have done so by developing a strong commercial orientation. In this field, the traditional university has already been eliminated as effective competition for the knowledge industries.

This is less true in other fields. Good work is being carried out by consultancy companies in such disciplines as geography, but here there *is* significant competition from the universities. For example, some are playing an important rôle in providing geographical information systems which enable organisations—both public and private—to discover quickly from computer screens how land is being used in the UK, what buildings are on it, and so on.

In social science research as a whole, competition from knowledge businesses is likely to be significant, especially in applied research.

(c) Consultancy

This is the one field where the universities and the knowledge industries both operate. In the universities, consultancy takes two forms.

First, there is freelance consultancy by individual academics or groups of them. Second, there is consultancy organised by the university itself.

Freelance consultancy has to be fitted in between other activities, often to the detriment of both. It is all too easy to be over-committed, to run out of time and to perform neither task well. This reflects a more general university problem—lack of professionalism—not so much in possessing too little technical expertise as in having too few office facilities and too little general business slickness—in the best sense of those words. I cannot prove this, but I suspect that supervision of postgraduate students suffers more than anything else in competition with consultancy.

Because freelances who are also university teachers and researchers have less time available, work often takes longer than it would do if it were carried out by professional consultants.

In our second category, where consultancy activities are set up by universities themselves—whether or not as separate businesses—they operate very much as do private consultants. The University of Salford has achieved a good reputation since it decided to establish consultancy activities as a way of offsetting a reduction in support from the University Grants Committee in the early 1980s. This is a legitimate activity for a university and can be a valuable one, especially in, for example, applied science, engineering, management and other social sciences where it keeps academics up-to-date with developments in the outside world and where their expertise allows them to make a useful contribution. There is, however, a danger that the traditional parts of the university will regard consultancy as a second-rate activity and try to discourage it. For, though many academics do not see consultancy as academically reputable, it may keep its practitioners more lively and more up-to-date than its detractors believe.

Organisation of University Consultancy

Even where consultancy is organised by the university, there can still be a problem in ensuring that those who engage in consultancy, in university teaching and in the supervision of students, divide up their time as they have contracted to do. But at the very least there is now an organisation behind the consultancy activity with a vested interest in seeing that this happens.

Establishing consultancy as an activity within the university tackles the problem posed by the minority of academics who, having accepted 'full-time' jobs in universities, then devote so much of their time to freelance consultancy that they give the university a bad deal. Some universities and business schools handle this issue well, with the Vice-Chancellor or Director insisting that consultancy can be taken on only with his or her agreement, but such an arrangement is not universal. Even where it exists, it is impossible to police it fully.

The rapid expansion of the knowledge industries in recent years has enabled academics in universities—freelance or not—to increase the amount of consultancy work they take on. It has led to an even more rapid increase in the amount of consultancy carried out by private-sector organisations—and some public-sector ones—outside the universities.

VI. CONCLUSIONS

The next decade must transform universities. Lest it be suggested that a decade is so long that there is no need for early change, we should remind ourselves that universities change very slowly. In any case, though it may be the next century before there has to be dramatic transformation in universities, for them to keep up with what is required, change in the 1990s will have to be both steady and cumulative. Not only in Britain, universities need to begin answering questions some of which, even 10 years ago, would have seemed far-fetched.

(a) *What* is a University?

First, *what* will a university be? The short answer is that it will become a base for a diverse set of people and activities, but I must expand on that.

Before I do I should explain that, to save space and to avoid irritating readers I shall, each time I use the word 'student', do so in as broad a sense as the context implies.

As I wrote this section, I realised that I was recreating from scratch the 'shamrock' organisation,[1] which is now seen as typical of businesses in the 1990s, not least in the knowledge industries. The shamrock has three parts—hence its name: a professional core, a contractual fringe and a flexible labour force.

The 21st-century university will have, as part at least of its professional core, a group of high-powered academics. Since their pay must be sufficient to retain them against competition from the knowledge industries, their numbers are likely to be relatively small, but each will have to see that his or her activities have an impact on far more people than at present. Otherwise, the finances will not balance. We are back with economies of scale.

Books and articles in journals will continue to be important ways of disseminating academic knowledge, but now supplemented by large databases from which computers will rapidly display on screens (and/or print out to take away) what the

---

[1] See, for example, Charles Handy, *The Age of Unreason*, London: Business Books, 1989, pp. 70-92.

reader wishes to see. So will television programmes, audio and video tapes and interactive computer systems which, having ascertained what students do not know, help them to learn it.

Such programmes will be produced by teams with one or more core academics in them, backed up by media experts of a kind only the Open University currently deploys on a significant scale. Some of the information and ideas thus disseminated will come from academic researchers, but others from work carried out by freelances with weaker or stronger links to universities, or by businesses in or on the fringe of the knowledge industries.

To earn their keep, academics in the 'core' must reach large audiences, national and international. These core academics will organise prestigious seminars for modest-sized groups of 'students', but will also communicate with larger groups of them. As consultants, they will talk with and advise technical specialists and businessmen who work both within and outside the knowledge industries. Because their time is limited and because technology will soon make it relatively easy and cheap, core academics will provide disseminated brain-power to more outsiders than ever before, while travelling less.

Academic 'Impresarios'?

Some academics will move the other way, becoming less specialised, particularly when working with continuing education courses. Especially with senior people, who will be both well-educated and well-informed, what will be required is not a specialist academic who claims total mastery over a subject area but an 'impresario', who brings in leading academics and practitioners—in the flesh, or on a screen—and presents them to 'students'. But there is more to it even than that: we know this because it is already beginning to happen. It is not simply a matter of putting visitors on stage—as with theatrical impresarios. The impresario must be a facilitator as well, enabling members of groups of students to learn from star speakers, and indeed each other, as much as is relevant to them in their own situations. This rôle of impresario/facilitator, while increasingly common in business schools, is quite foreign to most traditional universities, where colleagues are often positively discouraged from attending each other's lectures, and where the assumption is that most of the knowledge required by students is contained within the individual academic's brain.

Yet even all of this does not put what is happening broadly

[58]

enough. We are approaching a new Hollywood era. Some UK academics are television mini-stars already. So, even more, are international (or US) stars. This will become a very well-paid profession for those with internationally acceptable talent. There will, therefore, have to be programme producers as well as impresarios since knowledge is now being packaged. This really is 'show-biz'—and universities are hopeless at that!

More junior teachers and tutors will back up both the 'stars' and the educational consultants. The consultants' rôle will be to help each student to use personal contact with academics and with visitors from outside the university—as well as the growing stock of books, films, video-tapes and databases—to pursue his or her 'own' education as effectively as possible. Given the diversity of these sources of information, we should now call them 'knowledge banks'.

Some educational consultants and tutors may well be among the core of professionals in the university, though it is not clear exactly what kind of division of labour within the 'core' will develop. Perhaps educational consultants—even some tutors—will be more helpful to students if they do *not* come from the core, but from the fringe either of people in the knowledge industries or of freelances in the twilight zone between them and the universities. Using such people will give greater flexibility and, once universities recognise the need to provide continuing education, this could be important because student numbers may be more variable than at present. Especially in technical and professional fields, drawing on the penumbra will also ensure that university education is not out of date or remote from real-world practice. As I shall explain below, alumni have a particular part to play in this.

The challenge is that, to succeed, the 21st-century university must learn how to organise itself to make effective use of those who work in the fringe—contractual or freelance—and they should learn from one of the failings of British business schools at present. This is the difficulty most have in organising themselves to make best use of the knowledge and experience of outsiders—as visiting professors or fellows. So much so that one visiting professor recently suggested to me that the collective noun should be a 'disorganisation' of visiting professors.

The third element of the 'shamrock' organisation is the flexible labour force—flexible especially in the sense that many of its members will be part-time. Whether that kind of flexibility will be required in universities or not, universities will have to back up both those from the core and those from the fringe, employing first-rate administrators and having more marketing skill than ever before, to ensure effective competition with other universities and with knowledge companies seeking to take business from them.

Energy levels will have to rise too, for universities do not radiate energy. Too few academics appear committed. In their own way they may be, but can they generate as much drive as those outside universities? Academics appear to churn knowledge, just as civil servants, often at least as able, churn paper.

Continuing Education and the Universities

The growth of continuing education will progressively open large potential markets to universities. But, to capture them, universities will have to learn how to keep up with leading-edge practice, because this is precisely where competition with private-sector training businesses is likely to be keenest. The total market for continuing education is still so big that the universities will have to be singularly incompetent not to share substantially in it, but to do so will call for higher standards in administration and marketing—and probably in education and training themselves—than at present. We must never forget the 180,000 people in touch with the Open University. I *know* that the majority are not pursuing degree-level courses but the sheer number is impressive, compared with about 350,000 undergraduates and postgraduates in *all* other UK universities.

Measured by student numbers, any university worth its salt should find that those taking degrees by the 2000s will represent less than half the total. Since much continuing education will require students to devote relatively short periods of time to it in any one year—though spread over a long period—degree students will nevertheless account for a higher percentage of student days than of student numbers. When considering what is likely, we must remind ourselves that in 1987/88 London Business School and Manchester Business School obtained only 49 per cent and 21 per cent respectively of their funds from the University Grants Committee.

The Role of University Alumni

This leads to a key issue—the relationship between universities and their alumni. Even in business schools, which should know

[60]

better, students are rarely helped to treat their time in the school as part of their total career development. And once they leave the school, there is often little attempt to help them to develop as individuals, employees or indeed employers. Nor is there much effort to persuade a former student to see the school as the obvious source of his or her continuing education.

Even where a school (or a university) in the UK does try to keep in touch with alumni, the latter are usually seen as targets for a refined form of begging, not as people who will gladly turn to the school for continuing training or education. It is true that some former students are only too keen never to see their school or university again, but personal experience shows me that many positively *want* to be invited back for further courses. Most are not.

There is, however, an even more important rôle for alumni—as tutors or as educational consultants. The alumni of the university already know its ethos and understand its ways. They can therefore be the most valuable members of the network of insiders and outsiders which the 21st-century university must bring together, difficult though it may be to organise.

What virtually no-one, even in a business or professional school, seems to realise is that, viewed in the way a good consultancy practice would, every professional school—even most universities and polytechnics—are sitting on a potential gold-mine. From a much shorter client list of individuals and businesses, the average consultancy company would have established a large number of lasting and profitable professional relationships. With few exceptions, universities virtually throw away a valuable client list, as well as the goodwill of many alumni. This is only one lesson that a successful university will have to learn from the knowledge industries, but it may be one of the most important.

(b) *Where* is the University?

The second question which universities must begin to address is: *Where* will the university be? If its rôle is to provide resources of all kinds which both students and outsiders can tap, it will be most economic for the university's core academics, and its libraries, databases, stocks of films, video-tapes, and so on to be centralised. Students, businessmen, professionals and all others who want to learn will still meet on-campus but they will also meet each other off-campus, under their own auspices or those of the university. They will do so with or without help from academics—whether in the same room, or on television or tape. Loners will learn in their homes or offices.

The campus will survive, but must be much more permeable. It will be the place where at least some students spend some (even most) of their time in intellectual and social contact. But with cheaper computing and telecommunications facilities those off the campus (and even on it!) will communicate more easily and cheaply than ever with each other. In one sense, the university will continue to be where the campus is. In another, it will be wherever students are geographically, and that could well cover a large area.

As we move into the 21st century universities will also see themselves as providing large knowledge banks. Nor should access to these be restricted. *All* who want to learn should be encouraged to use these facilities—books and journals; films and video-tapes; and computers giving access to large databases or to teaching packages—whether formally attached to the university or not.

In the 1990s this may sound too much like science fiction; by the year 2000, even these predictions will be too timid.

(c) *What* Are Universities For?

The third question is: What are universities *for*? It may seem strange to put this question third, but we need some of the points made in answering the first two questions to deal with it. It may, indeed, seem strange to ask the question at all. Yet universities rarely do, and that is part of the problem.

The obvious answer is that the rôle of universities is to produce excellently educated graduates, but that is too shallow a response. Universities should give undergraduates, graduates and as many as possible of its other clients, in the Open University sense, three things.

First, they should generate curiosity—an interest not merely in the student's own specialism, but in others too.

Secondly, going beyond that, universities should encourage lateral, innovative thinking: today they too often produce analytical rather than creative minds. Since not all minds are capable of great originality, perhaps universities should do the currently unthinkable and insist that all new students, whatever their ages, should take psychological tests which indicate which of them are most likely to have, or to develop, creative minds.

[62]

Potential lateral thinkers should then be helped to develop that ability. Indeed, every student should be helped to develop his or her individual characteristics—a revolutionary notion in a university.

We now know a great deal about the different characteristics of human beings, and how to identify them. Some are creative thinkers, others more analytical, yet others men and women of action. Universities should build on that knowledge of personal attributes and should stop assuming—as they implicitly do—that all students are essentially similar and will develop in much the same way through an undifferentiated educational process. Putting an end to such thinking is presumably one thing educational consultants will do, the more so if they are brought in from the outside world and are not all full-time academics.

Thirdly, universities should arouse excitement in students and sustain it in both students and staff. They should set off a spark which stays for life: the kind of spark that gets one out of bed in the morning.

Organising Educational Processes

How should all this be achieved? The key task of the 21st-century university must be to organise educational *processes* which develop these characteristics in all students, which is why this *Paper* is essentially about processes of learning. Those processes must be judged not *only* in terms of numbers of degrees awarded but in more qualitative terms as well.

This is therefore where I see the emphasis in the alliances of talent established with knowledge businesses. Some may be general. For example, a university faculty or school—conceivably a whole university—may agree to collaborate with businesses in combining the best brains of the two organisations to develop news ways of teaching in new or old fields; to increase the quality and impact of research; to work out new ways of organising the faculty or school and of marketing its programmes; and so on.

Other ventures may be more specific. A university may link with one or more businesses to engage in research or con-sultancy. Or a new venture may bring together a university, a knowledge business and individuals or companies from the media to produce films, videos and/or other material for distance-learning programmes. The possibilities are endless. The important thing is to meet the needs of clients, whether students, businesses, other organisations or individual 'clients'.

In a world of continuous change the emphasis must always be on advancing knowledge and its understanding. A university should see each generation of students as standing on the shoulders of earlier generations, but not defensively or in a backward-looking way. And it must recognise that in future a generation of students will be linked to it over a much longer period. Each generation will know what is deposited in its own knowledge bank: each has a duty to make its own deposit, so that tomorrow's bank will be greater. Part of that duty—which is especially one for teachers and researchers—is to ensure that all in universities become, in C. P. Snow's splendid phrase, men and women with 'the future in their bones'.

The Approach to Research

We must now look more narrowly at research. Universities should topple orthodoxies. We should all assume that they will, even if those orthodoxies happen currently to be our own. But they should not topple orthodoxies in an iconoclastic way. Academics must believe that acquiring the ability to test ideas and evidence is the primary benefit of university learning, remembering, with Karl Popper, that all 'isms' are dangerous. Popper also rightly emphasises that intellectual honesty is vital. One of the best statements of his position is, for some reason, tucked away in a lengthy but striking footnote.

> 'Only if a student experiences how easy it is to err, and how hard to make even a small advance in the field of knowledge, only then can he obtain a feeling for the standards of intellectual honesty, a respect for truth, and a disregard of authority and bumptiousness. But nothing is more necessary today than the spread of these modest intellectual virtues.'[1]

Popper's notion of falsifiability[2] (or refutability) should be the watchword in research.

Popper argues that there is no knowledge 'which implies finality'. What we call knowledge, or science, or indeed social science, is 'information regarding the various competing hypotheses and the way in which they have stood up to the various tests'. In other words, at any time 'science' is made up of those hypotheses which tests have not falsified, or refuted, though later

[1] K. R. Popper, *The Open Society and its Enemies*, London: Routledge & Kegan Paul, 1945, Fifth Edition, reprinted 1990, Vol. 2, Ch. 11, note 6, pp. 283-84.

[2] *Ibid.*, p. 13. All quotations in the next paragraph come from p. 13.

some of the hypotheses may be refuted. Scientific statements 'must be refutable'. Indeed, in the 'empirical sciences . . . proofs do not occur, if we mean by "proof" an argument which establishes once and for ever the truth of a theory'.

Behind this view of research lies Ernest Gellner's argument that industrial society was made possible only because Western civilisation achieved the primacy of men with pens over men with ploughs and swords. 'The possibility of storing, organising and transmitting meaning by means of writing is as fundamental as the production and storage of wealth.'[1] It is a very long story, as Gellner shows, but if men with pens are set loose, new advance is possible. That is how old ideas are toppled, though today such men may wield not pens but computers.

In universities the conventional wisdom is, of course, that the performance of researchers is best judged by research findings published in 'refereed' journals and that research should (or at any rate often *will*) be carried out in parallel with teaching. The next question usually asked is: What guarantee is there that a good researcher will also be a good lecturer/tutor? The conventional answer is that enthusiasm for his research interests will enable even an incoherent teacher to get his message over. In fairness, I must add that most universities have taken considerable strides lately towards improving the communication standards of those who teach. My own twist to this argument is that developments in information and communication technology will progressively give students more access to high-quality material on films, etc., releasing less able teachers for other activities.

I still worry, though, whether the best way to guarantee competence as a teacher, tutor, or even educational consultant is to use publications as a proxy. This matters because the tradition that the potential academic should carry out research in a narrow field is manifestly not the way to produce polymaths, whether or not it may produce tolerably good teachers.

Businesses in the knowledge industries will apply commercial principles and give clients what they really want. That is why all those engaged in training and education will have to become more concerned with learning *processes* than universities ever have been. They will not be able to avoid looking much more carefully at what they are seeking to give students and how they are doing so. *In such a world, the universities' assumption that*

1 Ernest Gellner, *Plough, Sword and Book*, London: Collins Harvill, 1988, p. 276.

experience in research alone produces good teachers may finally be seen as false.

Looking specifically at this issue in a business school, as one example of professional schools, what is required of academics there is an unusual combination of pedagogic skills and an ability to analyse situations so as to throw light on possible solutions. This is done by shrewdly identifying for students the relevant parts of a considerable academic (and business) literature which teachers fully understand. Obviously, the latest research in business and professional schools should be adding to the weight and relevance of this literature. But it does not follow that those who can interpret and apply that literature should be denied esteem and, more seriously, promotion because they contribute little to research findings which they manifestly understand.

Dissemination

A further problem of academic research is that even when it is of high quality and worth wide dissemination, this does not always happen. Too many academics use unnecessary jargon which positively conceals thought, and I am far from convinced by the frequent rejoinder to criticism of jargon that research findings are perfectly intelligible to colleagues in the specialist field. Even if that is true, for non-specialists it is often only when jargon has been translated into normal language that the brilliance or banality of research conclusions becomes clear. While these criticisms of the use of jargon are well merited in most social sciences, I am open to persuasion that the same criticisms cannot be directed at the arts, natural sciences and technology, though I have my doubts about them as well.

The growth of the knowledge industries must have a beneficial effect here, with those in the 'real world' insisting that research findings appear in plain language. This will certainly be the case with the results of consultancy work by academics. I hope it will carry through to research. Where research has practical implications, increasingly well-educated businessmen will be impatient with badly presented findings. Impatient, that is, if the findings come to their notice in time.

For I have already noted the slowness with which research is often published. It is *not* necessary for all research to be reported, however late, in splendidly presented and bound volumes. What really matters to most specialists is what research findings *are*. A computer printout (or a display on a screen) giving an intelligible summary will be enough in many cases to tell other specialists what they want to know. If they need more, desktop publishing, or the ability to read more on a screen or printout, may meet their needs. Beyond that, if established publishers will not reverse the relationship between speed and aesthetics in publishing, the entrepreneurs of the knowledge industries must.

The impact of the knowledge industries on universities will therefore vary. It will be biggest where the two compete—as they will in offering continuing education courses and in consultancy. It will be least in, for example, undergraduate courses in arts subjects or in research with little obvious or immediate practical relevance.

In other words, what is often called the 'liberal arts' college *may* need to pay the least attention of any university institution to developments in information and communications technology. I have, however, emphasised the word 'may' because this is far from certain. As an example in the opposite direction, I call attention to the fact that in a British experiment which is seeking to improve the processes of education, not least by using information technology, the evidence points the other way. In schools in Letchworth, a small town about 20 miles north of London, teachers of children between the ages of 11 and 18 are finding that students of the humanities are the most enthusiastic users of computers, word processors, and so on.[1]

The Importance of Science

It is often suggested that the greatest danger in an educational system which makes considerable use of information technology is that it will produce uncivilised adults. Yet Karl Popper has pointed out that 'a "literary" education' is not the remedy since it 'may create its own peculiar kind of narrow-mindedness, its peculiar snobbery'.[2] In particular, Popper believes that no-one can be considered educated who does not understand the significance of scientific development. Though again tucked away in a footnote in *The Open Society and its Enemies*, Popper's argument cannot be more strongly or clearly put. Far from being a mere collection of facts about particular branches of the subject, science

'is one of the most important spiritual movements of our day. Anybody who does not attempt to acquire an understanding of this

[1] Information from personal interviews in schools involved in the Letchworth 'Education 2000' project.

[2] Popper, *op. cit.*, note 6, p. 283.

movement cuts himself off from the most remarkable development in the history of human affairs.'[1]

Indeed he believes that because they ignore this, 'so-called Arts Faculties ... have therefore become obsolete in their present form'.[2] He goes on:

'There can be no history of man which excludes a history of his intellectual struggles and achievements; and there can be no history of ideas which excludes the history of scientific ideas.'[3]

This too must be taken into account in 21st-century education which can thereby play a part, if only a small part, in bringing together C. P. Snow's two cultures.

Not that scientists are entirely spared. Popper is particularly critical of education in science 'which by some teachers is still treated as if it was a "body of knowledge", as the ancient phrase goes'.[4] His vision is of a science which 'can be taught as a fascinating part of human history—as a quickly developing growth of bold hypotheses, controlled by experiment, and by *criticism*'.[5]

'Taught in this way, as a part of the history of "natural philosophy", and of the history of problems and of ideas, it could become the basis of a new liberal university education; of one whose aim (*sic*), where it cannot produce experts, will be to produce at least *men who can distinguish between a charlatan and an expert.*'[6]

Popper's view was that this 'modest and liberal aim' was far beyond most arts faculties in the immediate post-war period. We have clearly made some progress since then, but arts faculties and liberal arts colleges could do much worse as we approach the 21st century than to make certain that they have brought themselves as far as possible to the position which Popper had already reached in 1945.

The Economics of 21st-Century Universities

It is difficult to say how the economics of 21st-century universities will work out. I do not waver in my belief that they will have to pay salaries similar to those paid in the knowledge industries. The aphorism that universities should pay twice the current salaries to half as many people must hold, in a general sense. In part, this must mean using technology to replace people. In part, it may mean employing less-skilled people to

---

[1] *Ibid.*, p. 283. [2] *Ibid.* [3] *Ibid.*

[4] *Ibid.*, note 6, p. 284. [5] *Ibid.* [6] *Ibid.*

back up the highest-paid members of the core. These may, indeed, constitute a flexible labour force in the sense that they are young, bright and gaining experience on their way to high-paid 'core' jobs either in universities or in knowledge businesses. They will be backed up by alumni and other outsiders, not as cheap labour but as links with the outside world. There will also be the large knowledge banks, open to all who want to learn, and there may be a further rôle for knowledge businesses in helping to establish and maintain these banks.

The key, however, must be for the university to use old-fashioned economies of scale to enable members of the core to reach large numbers of people, exploiting technology to the full. It must operate in a geographically dispersed market, even an international one, in order to offset the dangers already envisaged. We must not allow successful organisations in other countries to attract too many British students, though we must (and will) ourselves attract foreign students.

(d) Specialisation

One characteristic of businesses in the knowledge industries is that most of them choose to specialise. So should universities. Why should some not specialise in being first-rate at teaching, using both the best of the old methods and the best of the new ones which the knowledge revolution will make available? Why should others not specialise more—if not totally—in research, as research institutes in France and West Germany have done for years? Why should not still others concentrate on providing excellent continuing education programmes to meet rapidly growing demand? Or even on consultancy?

My concern may appear unnecessary since I have shown that about two-thirds of universities do concentrate on teaching, though their staff also carry out research, consulting, and so on. What I mean by specialising, however, is much more positive, with the organisation seen as one of the leaders of innovation in its chosen field, whatever that may be.

'Sticking to One's Knitting'

In private business, a way to excellence is today seen as 'sticking to one's knitting', being quite clear what one is good at and refusing to be drawn into activities which would divert the business from that. Universities should do the same. At present,

[69]

however, they cannot move significantly towards specialisation because they are regulated by the UFC, much as are public utilities in water, electricity or gas. Ranking them in terms of their performance in undergraduate *and* postgraduate teaching *and* in research *and* in the ability to obtain and manage funds for research, consultancy, and continuing education is unfortunate. It puts the emphasis on engaging in this spread of activities and on evaluation in traditional ways, especially through numbers of books or articles published in 'reputable' academic journals.

Not merely does the system described in Section III mean that there is no real incentive to discover what the 21st century requires of universities or what would benefit students. Attempts to do so are inhibited. The UFC acts as a proxy for students (who are not consulted at all) because, as we have seen, publications are used as a proxy for the general ability of university staff. Efforts *are* made to rank publications in terms of quality as well as quantity, but there is always a danger that quantity will win.

Even that is not the real point, which is about specialisation. To be approved by the regulator, a university has to give a convincing appearance of fitting the UFC's model. Even if appearance and reality actually match, it is a model which may or may not have been appropriate in the 1960s or 1970s but which *cannot* be the only correct model for the 2000s. It prevents a university being very good at a single activity which it believes it can perform best, insisting that all universities must cover a wide range of activities, even if that serves the nation less well than specialisation would. Worse still, it deters innovation. The best that this kind of regulation can ensure is high-level mediocrity. Anything else is a bonus—and one rarely provided.

The UFC gives little credit for innovation at precisely the stage in the development of the university system when innovation is desperately needed. It is not directing itself to discovering what the models for successful universities in the 21st century will be and ensuring that they are adopted.

The system must change but change will not be easily accepted. This is because in Britain—more perhaps than in any other country—there is a paradox. The general populace greatly respects the universities. So do members of the freelance fringe, even though they know the university's warts much better than does the outside world. For most people, universities are like 'good regiments'. Even the most successful senior manager in a clearing bank or multi-national corporation often does not have the same sense of his own organisation as he does of universities—especially Oxbridge.

(e) Status

Writing soon after the 50th anniversary of the Battle of Britain, an appropriate analogy might be 'Spitfire snobbery' among the Luftwaffe. German pilots shot down by the British during the Battle of Britain always claimed to have been downed by Spitfires, not Hurricanes. In a similar way, universities are seen by the British as Spitfires, never Hurricanes—as the *really* open-minded and prestigious learning places. (Actually, German pilots were not fair to Hurricanes. Spitfires were faster, but Hurricanes more manoeuvrable.)

Yet unless they change, perhaps the very status of universities will be their undoing. This is so even when an institution was originally set up to break the mould of university education. That was why University College, London was established in the 1840s, after the Reform Act—to break the monopolies of Oxford and Cambridge. Later, it too became 'grand'. In the same way, the pre-war university colleges in towns like Leicester, Nottingham and Exeter also became 'grand' and insisted on becoming universities. In the 1960s the Colleges of Advanced Technology became 'grand' too. Today, many polytechnics yearn to become universities and, if the present system survives, one day some politician will be daft enough to let them. It is 'grandness' which needs to be done away with.

My final point is this. We may find it hard to create the university of the knowledge society but, once we have done so, I see it as a holding company, with all kinds of subsidiaries. Some will succeed and some will fail. Yet that very ability to fail will give universities a greater ability to renew themselves than they now have. Some subsidiaries will come directly out of the university; others from knowledge businesses. Yet others will represent joint ventures between the two. The fact that these *are* subsidiaries of universities will give them kudos, even greatness, without, one hopes, conferring 'grandness'. They need legitimacy rather than respectability.

VII. POLICY

I have explained why, if one takes a long view, competition from knowledge businesses must have a significant impact on universities. I have gone on to argue that, if left to themselves, the knowledge industries may establish their own colleges and business schools; will certainly form alliances with universities; may even take some over. Given a couple of decades, the scene will be transformed.

We cannot, however, wait that long. What we need from the universities as we approach the 21st century is for them to offer stimuli to the rest of the knowledge society which will lead to the intellectual equivalent of economic take-off. There is good—as well as mediocre—brain-power in them. We must unlock it.

It is a matter of making best use of our resources. Aneurin Bevan, in 1944, pointed out that the UK had every reason to succeed since it was an island built on coal and surrounded by fish. Peter Hennessy recently commented:

> 'Of course it helps if you have coal and fish—though A. Scargill took care of one and the Icelanders the other. But the one fixed capital asset any nation possesses which cannot be depleted either by being used up or made redundant by a shift in the world economy—is good old grey matter.'[1]

Like the Japanese, the UK must base its future on 'grey matter'—on the realisation that brains are the only truly renewable resource. We cannot afford 'own goals' in policy-making where brain-power is concerned. We must somehow bring together the long-established virtues of the university, the innovations of technology and the growing strength of knowledge businesses. We must create a community of common citizenship dedicated to generating the intellectual take-off without which the UK will never be a full member of the international knowledge society of the 21st century.

The Secretary of State for Education and Science may be reluctant to intervene in a tricky field, but I believe that there are three steps which the Secretary of State can take which,

[1] P. Hennessy (1990), *op. cit.*

taken at the right moment, would speed up the process. I list them in ascending order of significance.

1. Degrees

As time passes and more knowledge businesses are in a position to do so, he should ensure that more organisations are enabled to award both undergraduate and postgraduate degrees. In the next few years, perhaps all that will be needed is for the CNAA to continue to encourage collaborative ventures in providing degree courses between polytechnics and knowledge businesses and for universities to collaborate with such businesses in the same way. This is a useful way of breaking down academic isolation, whilst introducing businesses to the desirable features which academic institutions do have and which should not be lost.

In due course, one hopes that the CNAA will positively encourage knowledge businesses to offer their own degree courses. If that does not happen the Secretary of State himself has the power to allow them to do so.

2. Salaries

All national university pay scales should be abolished and individual universities left to determine how many people, of what types and on what terms, they wish to employ given their financial position. This would make it easier for universities to recruit and retain good staff in competition with the knowledge industries.

Similarly, at least for *new* staff, there should be no question of tenure for life. Even in the more slowly changing world of the 1960s and 1970s, the granting of life tenure left universities with some individuals whose skills were no longer those which the university required; yet it had little or no leverage for persuading them that they should be retrained.

It is now no longer merely a matter of whether universities find it easy enough to attract, retain and if necessary retrain men and women with a knowledge of academic subjects. As technology develops, universities will need people with quite new skills—for example, for making films or television programmes, or in running video-conferences. More and more experts in good communication, in all senses of the word, will have to be recruited.

Ideally, no-one should be allowed to spend more than seven or eight years working full-time in a university without a spell of at least two years in a non-university occupation. This is probably too much to expect, though it would be right. At the very least, more flexible pay arrangements and the ending of tenure would move the universities in the right direction. Intellectual capital would circulate more freely and would be energised and revitalised—to the good of all.

I realise that most people appointed to academic posts are no longer given life-time tenure. But unless something can be done to eliminate tenure for those who already have it, we shall have to wait 20 or 30 years before there is the flexibility in the university job market that we already need.

I also realise that some universities, at least, are looking aggressively for the best academics they can persuade to work for them, so that there is some flexibility there.

I am strengthened in my views by Ernest Gellner's belief, already quoted, that 'the average professor ... can be replaced from outside the teaching profession with the greatest of ease and often with little, if any, loss'.[1]

It is not only that universities *need* continuous change and therefore renewal in their people, academic direction, skills, ethos and culture. This is only the demand side of the equation. The growth of knowledge industries will ensure that there is an adequate supply of more than competent people outside the universities able to move into them for spells in teaching, research and, *a fortiori*, consultancy.

3. Competition

While valuable, these changes will not go to the root of the question, which is how to pull the universities into the new millennium. Competition must be the answer. Organisations as set in their ways as most universities are do not change themselves unless given substantial encouragement to do so, or severe punishment if they do not.

But *what* change? The fiasco over the UFC's effort to operate a 'market system', by asking universities to bid for students and money, shows how hard it is to get universities to behave in new ways. Yet even what has proved impossible was itself inadequate. Universities were invited only to provide what the UFC believed was necessary, and bureaucrats who regulate organisations do not have the ability of free markets to foster innovation. Recent experience in Eastern Europe shows this clearly.

[1] Gellner, *Nations and Nationalism*, *op. cit.*, p. 36.

Indeed, it cannot be said too starkly: bureaucracies, whether political, administrative or educational, *cannot* innovate successfully. Officials have too little understanding of what is possible, because they include too few lateral and forward thinkers who can see what is necessary in a rapidly changing world. If they could they would not be bureaucrats. After all, even those *inside* universities who care about such things find it difficult to know what the future requires and they do, at least, understand education. For the next two decades, the changes needed will be rapid and fundamental. They can come about only through numerous experiments which no bureaucracy could hope to organise. We need a pluralistic system, not a centrally controlled one.

(a) Scholarships

We must therefore reduce the rôle of the Universities Funding Council, at most, to one of providing grants to students. The basis of university finance must be that universities obtain the funds required to sustain their teaching activities from students' fees so that students, not bureaucrats, determine which universities thrive. The proportion of the fee to be paid by students themselves, or their parents, and any subsidy to be provided by the State, could be varied as time passes. Any state subsidy should take the form of *state scholarships* for both undergraduate and postgraduate students. Their number, size and allocation to individuals could be dealt with as the residual rôle of the UFC, or directly by the Department of Education and Science. (In practice, the task would be so great that universities would have to help with the assessment of individual students.) We may note that a much smaller, but similar, scheme for postgraduates has been run successfully by the ESRC for several years.

Whether or not supplemented by grants or loans to cover the maintenance of students, state scholarships would replace the UFC's grants to universities. There would be real choice and real competition. Universities would have to explain more carefully than at present what they were offering students but, having done so, they would be free to design and re-design courses and introduce other activities without bureaucratic supervision from outside the university. The customer—the student—would be king; the supplier—the university—would be free to decide how best to serve him. That freedom must include the freedom to go out of operation. When the first university fails we should cheer, not mourn. Human capital must circulate if the knowledge society is to thrive.

Presumably students themselves, or their employers, would cover the cost of their continuing education, but in the 1991 Budget speech, the Chancellor of the Exchequer foreshadowed a scheme to offer tax relief to many such students from 1992. The individual student must, however, decide which university should receive his custom.

Student fees, plus any other fees which universities earn or donations which they attract, would also have to cover the cost of maintaining and developing libraries, in their extended rôle as knowledge banks.

(b) Research

The funding of research might pose a rather weightier problem. For the first few years, it might be most sensible for the Department of Education and Science to hand over the funds which the UFC currently provides to support research in universities to the Research Councils, which could then allocate the funds between universities.

The sum of money is substantial—around £1 billion per annum—but its function is not quite what it seems. There is also a story related to it.

When Kenneth Baker became Secretary of State for Education and Science, I was Chairman of the Economic and Social Research Council. On the day he arrived at the Department of Education and Science, I wrote to Mr Baker. I pointed out (as I did earlier in this *Paper*) that much of this large sum, which the (then) UGC paid to the universities to cover research by academics was, as it still is, notional.

It is notional in the sense that it represents pay for that part of the effort of university teachers which they are thought to devote to their own research. The convention is that university teachers are expected to spend some of their time—especially during vacations—working on research. Some do spend this notional amount of time, or more. Others spend less. That leaves open the question whether research financed in this way—much of which is completed but never published—is worthy of support: quite apart from the question whether those concerned might not obtain greater benefit both for themselves and their universities if they spent their time differently. I am raising again my doubts about the

UFC's implicit (if not indeed explicit) concept of a standardised academic working in a standardised university.

My suggestion to Mr Baker was this. A pay claim from university teachers was then being considered and I believed that university pay had fallen so far behind that of competing groups that there must this time be a substantial pay increase. I therefore suggested to Mr Baker that the UK should introduce a practice widely found in the USA. University teachers should be paid a basic salary only, for working from October to June each year. If this scheme had been introduced at the time of a substantial pay award, that would have meant no pay rise, or a small reduction, for those who took only the basic pay. Their time in the fourth quarter (July-September) would, however, have been entirely theirs, to use as they wished.

They might, however, be willing to run a Summer School, carry out other teaching or preparation duties for the university, or to help with administrative tasks. For this work, they would be paid an appropriate additional amount.

My assumption was, however, that many university teachers *would* want to spend the fourth term—or some of it—working on research and being paid for doing so. I suggested that for this to happen the academic in question would have to convince his or her university: (a) that he or she had feasible and useful research work in mind; and (b) after the event, that the research had led to a worthwhile result in the shape either of paper(s) written or of knowledge gained. Otherwise, the researcher would receive only the basic salary in future years. My aim was to give universities more control over the way their funds were used.

The reaction from the Department of Education and Science was that had they contemplated a substantial pay rise for university teachers, this might have been a worthwhile proposal, but that a substantial rise was not likely. In the event, there *was* a substantial pay increase but it took months to negotiate. By then the DES had 'forgotten' my suggestion.

If the UFC is abolished this proposal could be taken up again. Universities could use some or all of what used to be the notional amount paid to them to finance individual research in roughly this way, though this would now be done at the choice of the individual, not that of the UFC. This would link both teaching and research funds to the number of students.

I also hope that with greater freedom of this kind, universities would encourage more specialisation by individuals. Just as the

UFC pushes a standard university towards similarity rather than diversity, so the ethos of universities is itself too egalitarian. In part this is a matter of pay, which is why I want to see the end of national pay scales. In part, it results from an apparent determination among university teachers that there should be a standard academic, with each devoting a similar proportion of his or her time to teaching, research, administration, and so on. Far from agreeing to allow star researchers to specialise, and devote as much time as possible to high-class research which will give the university kudos, most academics hold that all members of each department should be given a similar amount of time for research, even though all are not equally able researchers. Allowing individuals to concentrate on what they do best to the good of the department or university ought to become standard practice, and perhaps introducing some of the less egalitarian ethos of knowledge businesses will help here too.

Incentives for Innovation

Given my criticisms of the performance of universities, it may appear illogical to suggest that we can now rely on them to transform themselves. My response would be that those who work in universities, as in other fields of endeavour, react to the incentives and controls within which they operate. We have seen that the UGC/UFC system has rewarded conformity to established traditions. Certainly, those at the centre have sought to induce the universities to give better value for money in teaching and higher quality in research, but only within established guiding beliefs and ways of operating. Innovation has rarely occurred, because it has rarely been sought. We shall never be certain what capacity for innovation there is in universities until they work within a system which encourages it—and that is what the changes I propose will do. I believe we shall be surprised by the amount of academic enterprise and ingenuity we can release if we are willing to try. At present, academics are engaged in an elaborate 'game' with the UFC, not in innovation.

Even if I am wrong, and there is no innovative talent in universities, that simply reinforces the case for opening them to influences from knowledge businesses. Whatever the latter may lack, it is certainly not an ability to innovate, for that accounts for their very existence.

While fully committed to the notion of a free-market solution, I accept that one disadvantage would have to be overcome.

Markets work well only if good information is easily available to customers. It would be necessary and, I believe, it would happen that newspapers and other media devoted more space than at present to discussing the way in which particular universities were choosing to develop and the benefits and disadvantages which each of them therefore offered to potential students.

Since this alone would not be enough, I should also like to see some of the money released by scaling down the UFC used to subsidise the publication of several 'Good University Guides' on the lines of publications like the *Good Food Guide*.

Given this, most students would be in a rather better position to choose between universities than they are at present.

4. Polytechnics

One criticism which will be levelled at sub-section 3 above is that it should apply to other higher educational institutions as well, especially polytechnics. The reason I have written about universities alone is that, given 'Spitfire snobbery', this is where change should begin. In principle, such a scheme could be extended to other higher educational institutions later. Indeed, it should be.

The demise of the UFC would have another advantage. With nobody responsible for regulating the university system there would be no good reason to be so restrictive in permitting use of the name 'University'. I object strongly to arguments from polytechnics that they should become universities under the present arrangement, because that would simply add even more institutions to the UFC system. Once it has gone, each institution should be allowed to call itself whatever it wants. There would undoubtedly be some oddities as there are in the USA but, with arrangements for providing better information, students (and others) would know which institutions were rated as 'better' and which 'worse', whatever they called themselves.

I am pleased to see that there are already changes in the relationship between universities and polytechnics. It goes without saying that there is competition for students between them, not least because the Education Reform Act of 1988 reduced the significance of the dividing line between the two parts of what has come to be known as the binary system— between the universities on the one side and the polytechnics and other higher education colleges on the other. The reform act made the two parts of the system less distinct by giving autonomy to polytechnics and other higher education colleges and removing it from local authorities. There is now talk of giving polytechnics the power to award degrees. The moves by the UFC to ensure that universities educate more students at a lower average cost also makes the financing arrangements for universities more similar to those for polytechnics. Indeed, talks on funding methodology between the UFC and the body which finances polytechnics are now planned.

John Stoddart, Director of Sheffield Polytechnic, looks forward to a unitary system of higher education. Speaking to a conference on the Management of Higher Education at Manchester Business School early in 1991 he said:

'The foundation is now laid for a unitary system of higher education encompassing, say, 80 or 90 major institutions with consistency of funding methodology, quality assurance procedures, accountability and reporting relationships. A *unitary* system would in no way imply a *uniform* system—convergence of the two existing systems will, I believe, lead to a much more diverse and differentiated system than at present with a mix of institutions with different missions—some research universities, others more sharply focussed on teaching, on applied research and consultancy, on access—*and* with different funding dependent on the particular mission and performance.'[1]

Professor Stoddart made no mention of knowledge businesses but did show that, quite apart from the impact which knowledge businesses are bound to have on universities, the polytechnics will provide another major challenge to universities.

I would, of course, argue that if John Stoddart is right the polytechnics also must look to challenges and opportunities posed by the knowledge industries. A great deal of this *Paper* therefore applies as much to polytechnics or colleges of further education as to universities. Only the biggest and best institutions—whatever they are called—will be able to engage in large-scale collaboration with the knowledge industries, though smaller-scale collaboration will also be valuable and should be encouraged. The joint ventures of the knowledge society should vary in both scale and purpose.

That is why the second part of the title of this *Paper* is: 'A New Republic of the Intellect'. It emphasises that the knowledge society is for all with intellectual curiosity and staying power. It

[1] John Stoddart, 'Marketing of Higher Education': unpublished paper to a conference on the Management of Higher Education, Manchester Business School, 9-11 January 1991.

has overtones of Plato and, given his doubts about Plato's commitment to a genuinely open society, even more of Popper. It suggests both equality and common citizenship among a substantial body of those who have both intellect and a concern with its distribution, circulation and enrichment. Above all, in the new Republic of the Intellect there can no longer be 'divine rights of kings' for universities. This is axiomatic. Status will depend on performance and will have to be earned. That is all to the good.

QUESTIONS FOR DISCUSSION

1. Discuss the rôle of knowledge businesses in the modern economy.

2. Consider Ernest Gellner's contention that 'the average professor can be replaced from outside the teaching profession with the greatest of ease and often with little, if any, loss'.

3. What lessons can universities learn from the way knowledge businesses are organised?

4. How valid is Toffler's claim that failure to diversify education within the present system will lead to the growth of alternatives outside it?

5. How should university education be redesigned to make best use of developments in information and communications technology, especially in making 'lifelong learning' a reality?

6. What impact will the growth of knowledge businesses have on the argument that only greater government spending on it can 'save science'?

7. How should universities go about creating 'learning communities' of students, alumni and the intellectually aware?

8. Discuss the opportunities and problems which video-conferencing will provide for universities.

9. Is three or four years spent on writing an academic thesis the best training for a university teacher? If not, what would be?

10. How far and how should arts and social science students be introduced to scientific thinking, which Popper has

called one of the most important spiritual movements of our day?

11. Discuss the argument that a system in which (as in the UK) a central body oversees the development of all universities is as doomed to failure as have been the command economies of Eastern Europe.

SELECT BIBLIOGRAPHY:
READINGS FOR FURTHER STUDY

History and Philosophy

Carswell, John, *Government and the Universities in Britain*, Cambridge: Cambridge University Press, 1985.

Gellner, Ernest, *Nations and Nationalism*, Oxford: Basil Blackwell, 1983, especially Chapter 3.

———, *Plough, Sword and Book*, London: Collins Harvill, 1988, especially Chapters 2, 6, 7 and 8.

Popper, Karl R., *The Open Society and its Enemies*, London: Routledge & Kegan Paul, 1945, especially Vol. 1, Chapter 1 and Vol. 2, Chapter 11 (including note 6 on pp. 283-84) and Chapter 23.

Rudd, Ernest, *A New Look at Postgraduate Failure*, Windsor, Berks.: Society for Research into Higher Education and NFER-Nelson, 1985.

Futures

Drucker, Peter, *The New Realities*, London: Mandarin Paperbacks, 1989, especially Chapters 12-16.

Toffler, Alvin, *Future Shock*, New York, Toronto and London: Bantam Books, 1970, especially Chapters 7, 12, 17 and 18.

———, *Powershift*, New York, Toronto and London: Bantam Press, 1990, especially Chapters 6-8.

Individuals and Institutions

Hague, Douglas (ed.), *The Management of Science*, Basingstoke and London: Macmillan, 1991, especially Chapters 1, 2 and 3.

Illich, I., *Deschooling Society*, Harmondsworth, Middlesex: Penguin Books, 1971.

Kolf, D., *Experimental Learning*, Englewood Cliffs, New Jersey: Prentice Hall, 1984.

Smith, Robert M., *Learning How to Learn*, Milton Keynes: Open University Press, 1983.

Learning Systems

Beer, Stafford, *The Heart of Enterprise*, Chichester, New York and Toronto: John Wiley, 1979, especially Chapters 5, 7, 8, 9, and pp. 457-67.

Morgan, Gareth, *Images of Organisations*, Beverley Hills, London and New Delhi: Sage Publications, 1986, especially Chapter 4.

Schon, Donald, *Beyond the Stable State*, London: Temple Smith, 1971, especially Chapters 5 and 6.

OF RELATED INTEREST

Perestroika in the Universities

Elie Kedourie

Classical liberals have long argued that the independence of the universities from the state is endangered by over-reliance on government funding. In *Education for Democrats* (1964) Professors Alan Peacock and Jack Wiseman questioned whether the Robbins Committee was correct in supposing that university independence was assured if student fees comprised only 20 per cent of income. They advocated an alternative system of funding based on vouchers and student loans. The same theme was pursued by Crew and Young in *Paying for Degrees* (1977). More recently Professor H. S. Ferns took up the cudgels on behalf of university independence in *How Much Freedom for Universities?* (1982). He pointed out that until the mid-nineteenth century universities lived wholly on fees, endowments, donations and the sale of services. Reliance on state funding grew steadily through the 1930s but it was not until the 1963 Robbins Report that the balance changed dramatically. Professor Ferns warned that by the early 1980s the University Grants Committee had already turned into a controlling bureaucracy imposing on the universities a rigid homogeneity incompatible with the purposes of higher education.

Professor Kedourie's *Perestroika in the Universities* is the latest in this long line of IEA studies revealing the dangers of over-reliance on state funding. The Education Reform Act enforces tight official control over all aspects of university life, despite amendments in Parliament. Accused of being cartels of producer interests, of charging unnecessarily high 'unit costs', of giving too low a 'social return' on taxpayers' investments, universities now face a degree of central control over their activities reminiscent of the absolutism of an earlier Europe. Professor Kedourie argues that each university is *sui generis* and that the Government's imposition of central control runs clean counter to their declared aim of greater autonomy. Councils and Committees proliferate and the Committee of Vice-Chancellors and Principals works in unholy harmony with the DES.

ISBN 0-255 36257-9

£5.00

Obtainable from:
IEA Health and Welfare Unit
The Institute of Economic Affairs
2 Lord North Street, Westminster
London SW1P 3LB
Telephone: 071-799 3745
Fax: 071-799 2137

Europe's Constitutional Future

It is commonly recognised that Europe is going through its most profound period of change since the end of the Second World War. Furthermore, the changes are of such clear benefit that they have justly been greeted without reserve whether it be the advent of political freedom and the shift to the market economy in Eastern Europe or the putting in place of the Single Market in the European Community or the initiation of talks designed to bring about closer integration between the Community and the countries of the European Free Trade Area.

This volume follows an earlier volume of papers on Europe produced by the IEA entitled *Whose Europe?* and is part of the IEA's increasing programme of work on European topics. Enhancing political and economic co-operation in Europe is a top priority for all governments in Europe including Britain. The papers in this volume are designed to widen the debate on policy options in respect of institutional aspects of economic and political union in Europe.

CONTENTS

IEA Readings 33

ISBN 0-255 36237-4

£8.95

The Institute of Economic Affairs
2 Lord North Street, Westminster
London SW1P 3LB
Telephone: 071-799 3745